Book Review

Success: Live a Life Worth Living provides the ultimate integrated biblical explanation of what it means to pursue success from God's perspective. This is not just a book about success – it is a transformative exploration of how Scripture defines success, far removed from the world's superficial standards. Dr. Stubblefield masterfully weaves together a profound exegetical understanding of Scripture with a rich grasp of biblical narratives, historical contexts, and theological principles, offering a deep and practical framework for believers who want to align their pursuit of success with God's wisdom.

What sets this book apart is its ability to educate, illuminate, and challenge. It is a work that not only equips the reader with sound biblical doctrine but also inspires practical application – calling believers to examine their walk with Christ in light of God's revealed truth. Dr. Stubblefield skillfully integrates key biblical themes such as trust, perseverance, focus, ontological truth, spiritual gifts,

Christian suffering with trials, bringing clarity and depth that is often misunderstood in today's culture.

After 45 years of theological study, I found this book to be profoundly helpful in clarifying theological issues that had confused me over the years. The depth of scholarship and clarity in explaining complex theological concepts make this book invaluable for any believer serious about deepening their understanding of biblical success.

Dr. Stubblefield's insights provide a compelling, biblically sound guide for anyone serious about aligning their pursuit of success with the heart and wisdom of God. With every chapter, one gains a renewed sense of conviction and encouragement to live out biblical success in its fullest sense. I wholeheartedly endorse this book as an essential resource for mature believers who desire to think deeply, live faithfully, and pursue success as God defines it.

Gary Charles Patterson, M. Div., Th. M., D.D., MCC
Theologian, Leadership Consultant, Master Coach

SUCCESS
Live A Life Worth Living

A Biblical Perspective for Defining,
Pursuing, and Achieving Success

Table of Contents

Table of Figures

DEDICATION

This book is dedicated to my oldest sister, Regina Stubblefield-Thomas, who lived her life to the fullest, giving more than she received, conquering every challenge with perseverance, and maintaining remarkable faith in God as she combated the challenges of cancer with extraordinary courage.

FORWARD

On the journey of life, humanity encounters trials and triumphs. These trials test our resilience, but as believers in Jesus Christ, we are called not to let these challenges overshadow the triumphs of living a life of significance. Through my own journey, from surviving in challenging circumstances to achieving worldly success and ultimately discovering the significance of living for God, I have come to understand that true success is found in glorifying God and serving others.

With over 40 years of experience as a retired military officer, research scientist, regulatory compliance officer, and pastor-teacher, I am fully committed to living for the glory of God and making a Kingdom impact that echoes both now and for eternity. This commitment shapes my perspective on what it means to live a life worth living, a perspective masterfully communicated in this book by Dr. Cedrick Stubblefield Sr.

Dr. Stubblefield, a trusted and faithful servant leader at Covenant Community Church, where I have the privilege of serving as pastor, embodies the principles he so eloquently outlines in this book. His willingness to evaluate areas of need and take initiative in ministry, using his SHAPE for ministry, makes him a living testimony of what he writes. What God has done in his life, He can do for you.

In *Success: Live a Life Worth Living*, Dr. Stubblefield offers a biblical perspective for defining, pursuing, and achieving true success. He masterfully outlines the need to remeasure success, pointing us toward significance rather than worldly accolades. He encourages readers to trust God, persevere through challenges, focus on meaningful priorities, and cultivate the unique gifts and talents God has entrusted to us.

Drawing from his personal life experiences and scriptural truths, Dr. Stubblefield provides timeless wisdom that empowers believers to live lives pleasing to God. This is not a survival guide or a step-by-step manual for worldly success; it is a call to elevate your existence by aligning with God's purpose. His insights are simple, actionable, and relevant, regardless of where you are on your journey.

As someone who has seen firsthand how Dr. Stubblefield's life and leadership have impacted others, I can confidently say this book is a must read. It challenges us to move from mere survival to living with purpose, significance, and impact. It invites us to seek, know, and trust God in all things, propelling us to discover the true meaning of success.

Prepare to be inspired and transformed. As you read these pages, your perspective on success will shift, leading you to focus on what matters most and motivating you towards a life that ends with God saying, "Well done." This book is a transformative journey, one that will encourage you to embrace your God-given purpose and live a life worth living.

~ Dr Earl Grant Jr.,
Pastor and Founder
Covenant Community Church
San Antonio, Texas

ACKNOWLEDGEMENTS

Thanks be to God, which giveth us the victory
through our Lord Jesus Christ.
1 Corinthians 15:57

Thanks to my team of readers who reviewed this book to ensure its biblical accuracy, content flow, and universal readability.

Cedric Lang, my writing mentor, encouraged me yet again to publish my thoughts on true success. Every personal story contained in this book is a response to his challenge to connect with the reader with transparency.

Keron Long, my philosophical sparring partner, is truly gifted in the art of refining reality through the lens of the word until God's truths are revealed.

Dr. Gary Patterson, my scholarly coach, is an amazing thinker and communicator who is gifted to bring complex biblical truths to life in very simple and practical ways.

Dr. Aleck and Arnita Brown, a modern-day example of Aquila and Priscilla – a faithful couple you will read about in chapter 6 – are prolific students and teachers of the gospel.

Cheryl Craver, my social expert and sister, has the gift of hospitality and people advocacy. She has an inherent ability to connect and communicate with a wide spectrum of people, from toddlers to college professors.

INTRODUCTION

This book is an extension of *SALVATION: A Journey from Death to Life* where we examine the doctrine of salvation, God's plan for man's redemption, from the garden to glory. In the pages that follow, we build upon the principles of salvation, striving for the high aspiration of living our best life. In hopes of obtaining a sound understanding of our inherent role in the physical occupation of this world, we explore principles of the doctrine of Christian service.

What if we knew ourselves and others the way God knows us? The world would be significantly different. Everyone would be infinitely familiar with who they are and what they have the potential to achieve. Perfect knowledge of self would fuel our passions, stretch our imagination, and perfect our performance in all things. The world could rid itself of poverty, hunger, diseases, wars, and political strife. Instead, life is a journey of self-discovery where we strive to overcome the limitations – either natural, self-imposed, or levied by others – that would otherwise prevent us from becoming competent and confident in our abilities.

We, as George Santos suggested, should be careful not to fixate on answering "the secondary question What ought I to do? without having answered the primary question What ought to be?" (Santayana 1905). Discovering who we are and understanding our capabilities requires self-reflection. Blind pursuits and aimless living inevitably lead to less productive paths. They lead to detours and deviations that extend our journey and waste our most precious commodity, time.

We are all reservoirs of gifts and talents, a storage of untapped potential. We have within us the power and aptitude to change our environment in positive and impactful ways. During the precious, yet limited, time God has graciously bestowed, hundreds, thousands, and even millions can become better people after experiencing the love of God we demonstrate through the gifts and talents we employ in His service.

The love of God propels us to seek, know, follow, obey, and trust Him in all things. We are God's creation, and fulfilling our God-given purpose is the quintessential definition of success. How profitable is it to live our lives in pursuit of human affirmations? Is it profitable to gain the entire world and lose our soul (Mark 8:36)?

How much more effective would we be if every believer committed themselves to perfecting their God-given gifts? The value of every breath a believer takes is measured in how lives are changed because we are still breathing. The believer who defines success in terms of living life God's way, according to His will, and in pursuit of His purpose, discovers true success. Those who understand and acts upon the fact that God desires everyone "to be saved, and to come unto the knowledge of the truth" (2 Timothy 2:4), will with their last breath be able to say, "I have lived a life worth living."

But I keep under my body, and bring it into subjection: lest that by any means, when I have preached to others, I myself should be a castaway.

1 Corinthians 9:27

Chapter 1

REMEASURE SUCCESS

Humanity is driven by the need for success. Although the definition of success varies, everyone aims for it. We desire to be influential, popular, sought after, the first, the best, and above all accepted. Our motives for success are the same, independent of profession, culture, or practice. Athletes sacrifice their free time to train for it. Colleges and trade schools are filled with ambitious souls credentialing themselves for it. Some take shortcuts and fast-track their way to it. Yes, whether we work hard or sell our souls for it, we all seek the gratification of success.

In fact, we are wired from birth to chase success. We are celebrated for taking our first step and speaking our first discernable word. With this encouragement, we advance our auditory and motor skills. Inevitably, we discover our ability to control adult behavior by crying and the actions of other children by biting. The success we achieve in influencing outcomes emboldens us to continue our self-centered conduct.

Self-centered success, however, tends to be short lived and may not constitute "true" success. Parents usually learn the cries of their children and respond based on need rather than manipulation, and the habit of biting other children is met with less than desirable consequences. This leads us to question whether success gained through nefarious means is real success.

Furthermore, the pursuit of success can cause us to underappreciate our failures, an idea that reminds me of something my grandmother once cautioned me. "Some fights are worth fighting even if you lose and some aren't worth fighting even if you win," she admonished. This statement defines success relative to the greater good rather than one's personal satisfaction. The noteworthiness of an achievement attained upon a moral high ground is rarely, if ever, disputable. This is true success.

SEEK TRUE SUCCESS

True success is not defined by our status, notoriety, nor accomplishments. True success is enduring and can be characterized not just by what we achieve but by *how* we achieve it. David, the shepherd boy who would be king, was successful by every human measure. He is known for subduing 10,000 Philistines, a bear, a lion, and a giant. Yet, his achievements are not limited to what he accomplished with his hands.

Principled Success

King David failed often, and his failures can be counted among his greatest accomplishments. David's failures inspired him to become one of the world's greatest psalmists. By all accounts, history should have cast him – the man who orchestrated the murder of his mistress' husband – as a villain. However, the authenticity of his repentance overshadowed the heinousness of his acts.

David's interactions with Saul, his predecessor, stand as the embodiment of my grandmother's wisdom. When faced with opportunities to assassinate Saul and take the throne, he taught us that some things are worth doing even if we fail, and some things aren't worth doing even if we succeed. David chose the latter and refused to seize the throne as advised by his overzealous soldiers. In this principled moment of inaction, David established reverence for the reigning king and exemplified the sentiments of his song of thanksgiving (1 Chronicles 16:22), "Saying, 'Touch not mine anointed and do my prophets no harm.'"

The experiences of David exemplify a natural dichotomy between success and suffering; the latter is most often deemed tantamount to failure. Those who suffer are rarely considered successful, and successful people aren't generally expected to suffer. True success, however, cannot be realized without suffering, if only through sacrifice. Pain and sacrifice are the only acceptable currency when shopping for success. Suffering and success are inseparable. When cultivated by sacrifice and a commitment to learn and grow, failure invariably leads to success.

When my wife, Tamico, and I were young and in pursuit of our purpose in life, she elected to take a few college courses. It didn't go well. She signed up for two courses and failed them both. The failure shook her, and she began to speak what had been spoken to her, "College is just not for me."

Giving up or quitting because things are difficult was a foreign concept to me, so I gave her my best bit of advice. I told her, "Failure is not an option." I believed in her when she couldn't believe in herself. I didn't want failure to define her. As I saw it, she needed to change the narrative. Perhaps I could have been more understanding, but I was far less sympathetic in my youth; but it worked.

She took on the challenge and became an excellent student. Failing the courses simply shined a light on the areas she needed to fortify and gave her a strong appreciation for the need to prioritize and focus on studying for success. With an iron focus, she plowed through course after course with an exceptional academic record. She was determined not to finish with failure. No. Her failure catapulted her to success.

Consequential Success

You can imagine how proud I was when Tamico obtained her degree. She didn't stop there;

she now holds a Masters and Doctorate in nursing and is planning her next academic pursuit. Although degrees are significant achievements, the true success in Tamico's story is the countless number of people she has helped in improving their health and how she has demonstrated the love of God through her gift.

Those who achieve success, or reach a personal goal, discover that success tends to evolve into another venture marked by the next desired achievement. Trapped in an endless quest to realize our potential, success becomes more temporal than triumphal. Perhaps, the way we view success can get in the way of success.

Knowing and taking personal responsibility for the consequences of success makes the difference between success and failure clearly distinguishable. What if we judge success on its consequential merits rather than the rudimentary value that comes with accomplishing tasks, goals, aims, and achievements? The pain or relief, anger or joy, suffering or peace, and constraint or freedom our accomplishments produce in others should be the central criteria for defining success.

Jesus, in one of His parables about the Kingdom of God, illustrated how small things can make a significant difference. He said, in Luke 13:19, the Kingdom of God can be compared to "a grain of mustard seed, which a man took, and cast into his garden; and it grew, and waxed a great tree; and the fowls of the air lodged in the branches of it." God seeds us, the garden of the world, with gifts to grow and produce fruit. These gifts are the tools we need to branch out towards our best life, pursuing our dreams, aspirations, and purpose. Even those we esteem the least can expand their capacity to benefit others through their gifts.

True success is measured in terms of what we can achieve relative to our potential. Every good and perfect gift comes from above and is given to us to live life in a manner that maximizes our time, energy, and resources in service to others. When people change, everything changes. When we are successful at serving others, consciouses are awakened, cultures are shifted, and civilizations are advanced.

It is possible to be an heir to estates, influence, and even respect, but not true success.

True success is forged over time, preparation, and effort; it cannot be inherited. Hence, we say success is achieved. Those who labor with deliberate and persistent purpose will find success waiting at each milestone of their journey. These way-point victories, whether big or small, should never be underestimated but celebrated at a level commensurate with the achievement. Don't reserve your celebration for graduation, celebrate each class (or test) successfully completed. True success never really culminates; it is a series of failures and accomplishments in life's journey to please God and serve others.

LOVE ABOVE ALL THINGS

But the end of all things is at hand: be ye therefore sober, and watch unto prayer. And above all things have fervent charity among yourselves: for charity shall cover the multitude of sins. Use hospitality one to another * without grudging.

1 Peter 4:7-9

The Bible encompasses God's plan for humanity. In it, God outlines His purpose, vision, and mission for us. Jesus summarized this purpose in Matthew 22:38 when He identified the greatest commandment, to love God. In the next verse, we find His vision for us, to love our neighbors. Finally, He challenges us with our mission in Matthew 28:19. We are to make disciples, baptize them, and teach them. Gifts and talents are the tools God bestowed upon believers to abide in His love, express His love and spread His love to those in need of salvation.

Love is the primary catalyst that drives God's actions towards humanity. It is more than just an attribute of God's character but inherent to His person; God is Love. When God extends His love towards us, He gives us Himself. He is the greatest gift given to mankind, and by extension, there is no greater gift than Love. Before we can master the gifts, talents, and tasks God empowers us to accomplish, we should strive for mastery in love and actualize it in everything we do.

Every good and perfect gift comes from God, yet all are subordinate to love. God spread His love abroad in our hearts by the Holy Ghost (Romans 5:5). The type of love that compels a person to lay down their life for a friend is truly incomprehensible and cannot be exceeded (John 15:13). Love empowers believers to respond to every situation in a manner consistent with Christian character.

Without Love, we have no hope of offering someone the right side of our face when someone hits us on the left as expressed by Jesus in Luke 6:29. As extreme as it may sound, this is exactly what Jesus did the night before His crucifixion. He did not so much as enter a verbal confrontation with His accusers. The power of love is demonstrated in our ability to love our neighbor as we love ourselves (Matthew 19:19). The unique nature of God's love challenges us to love our enemies and do good to those who hate us (Luke 6:27). God gifts us with His love to do for others what He has done for us. As Paul explained in Romans 5:8, "God *demonstrated* His love toward us, in that, while we were yet sinners, Christ died for us."

The Greatest Gift of All

God not only empowers us to love, but He empowers us to love as He does. What a magnificent gift. It is the central gift around which all other gifts orbit. Whether we have the gift of language, prophecy, understanding, knowledge, faith, benevolence, or selflessness, none are superior to love (1 Corinthians 13:1-3). Paul states this in the most certain terms in 1 Corinthians 13:13, "And now abideth faith, hope, and *love,* these three; but the greatest of these is *love.*

An unwavering faith has the power to move mountains, yet it is subordinate to love (1 Corinthians 13:2). Imagine that.

- We are justified by faith (Rom 5:1).
- Our hearts are purified by faith (Act 15:9).
- We are children of God by faith (Gal 3:26).
- We live by faith (Rom 1:17).
- We stand by faith (2 Cor 1:24).
- Christ dwells in our heart by faith (Eph 3:17).
- We have access to grace by faith (Rom 5:2).
- God's power keeps us by faith (1 Peter 1:5).
- Mountains are moved by faith (Matt 17:20).
- We have victory over the world by faith (1 Jn 5:4).

Faith is vital to salvation. In fact, those who come to God must believe that he exists and rewards those who diligently seek him (Hebrews 11:6). So, how then can love be greater than faith?

Paul helps us with this question. In Galatians 5:6, he states that "In Christ, neither circumcision availeth anything, nor uncircumcision; but faith which worketh by love." There's no natural thing we can either do or not do to gain access to

God. Faith is the only authorizing agent for those who aspire to abide in Christ, and even this faith is perfected by love. If we have faith, it is because of Love.

If we have hope, it is also because of Love. Hope is the fruit of salvation. Love "beareth all things, believes all things, hopeth all things, endureth all things" (1 Corinthians 13:7).

- Hope is an anchor for our soul (Heb 6:19).
- Hope maketh not ashamed because of love (Rom 5:5).
- Jehovah is the God of hope (Rom 15:13).
- We have a living hope (1 Peter 1:3)
- We rejoice in the hope of salvation (Rom 12:12).
- We hope in God for the resurrection (Acts 24:15).
- We are saved by hope (Rom 8:24).

Our hope is inextricably tied to our faith. Jesus died so our "faith and hope might be in God" (1 Peter 1:21). We "wait for the hope of righteousness by faith" (Galatians 5:5). We have hope because we have faith. How can one expect to have hope for what they don't believe? How can we continue to hope for something when our faith is overcome by doubt?

Faith and hope are essential to our relationship with God. Without faith, it is impossible to please God (Hebrews 11:6) and hope is our strong defense over fear and sorrow. Yet, our greatest gift and our greatest challenge is love.

Love Fervently

Peter, in 1 Peter 4, begins by encouraging believers to relate to Christ by embracing his willingness to suffer and forsake the sin of our old life and live according to God in the spirit (vv. 1-7). Next, he echoes the words of Paul and says, "above all have fervent charity [or love] among yourselves (v8). Fervent love, he continues, "shall cover a multitude of sins." The word fervent here is from the Greek word *ektenés,* which means to stretch out, to make completely taut. Fervent love is not reserved or relaxed; it is fully extended. Peter encourages us to love without reservation. God's love is at its best when we are stretched to our breaking point.

Fervent love should not be taken lightly or underestimated; it is extremely demanding work. It demands that we love outside of our comfort zone. Believers must interact lovingly with others regardless of past sin and character flaws. In fact, fervent love can be recognized through acts of compassion; it covers faults, buries transgressions, and releases those who are bound by the offenses people have committed against us. Every believer is empowered with the power to exercise the love that covers all sin (Proverbs 10:12).

Fervent love for one another cannot happen without God's love working in us and through us. How can it when God is Love? God's love is amazing and sacrificial. It is the greatest gift of all.

God, sparing no expense, fully extended His love towards us when He purchased our salvation through the death of His son. Thankfully, His resolute power to love unconditionally resides within us. In this, we know that we have been empowered to put on Love, above all other virtues, which binds us together in perfect unity (Colossians 3:14).

True success for disciples of Christ is measured by love's pervasiveness in the decisions we make and the actions we take. Jesus said in John 13:33, "A new commandment I give unto you, that ye love one another; as I have loved you." The next verse tells us that the love believers have for one another evidences our relationship with Christ.

Therefore, the greatest success in life is mastering the greatest gift, love.

Figure 1.   Fervent Love is Stretched Love

Note: Image generated using Copilot from prompt "black and white image of heart being tugged with ropes." (OpenAI, December 31, 2024)

PLEASE GOD IN ALL THINGS

As every man hath received the gift, even so minister the same one to another *, as good stewards of the manifold grace of God. If any man speak, let him speak as the oracles of God; if any man minister, let him do it as of the ability which God giveth: that God in all things may be glorified through Jesus Christ, to whom be praise and dominion for ever and ever. Amen.

1 Peter 4: 10-11

15

Peter established love as the number one priority of God's gifts before shifting to the purpose of all gifts. God gives believers gifts to minister to one another according to His design (v. 10), and if we do, He will receive the glory (v. 11). God is exalted when we use our gifts to minister or serve one another as the Spirit leads, doing so not as a mere responsibility or duty but from the heart as Psalm 119:10 states, "With my whole heart have I sought thee: O let me not wander from thy commandments."

The Psalmist goes on to say in verse eleven, "Thy word have I hid in mine heart, that I might not sin against thee." He made a conscious decision to seek and obey God. The verses that follow suggests that he was committed to pleasing God in all his ways. His passion for serving God, which led him to rejoice in Him, meditate on His precepts, delight in His statutes, and long for His judgments, is undeniable.

Be Passionate

Passion, an intense, driving feeling or conviction, is a gift as well as a skill. Persistence tends to come easy when we pursue our passion. Every passion, however, will inevitably encounter roadblocks, which will force detours along the path to success. What do we do when our passion-fed persistence is met with limited time, resources, and opportunities? Should we forsake it? No, of course not. In times like these, our focus shifts to the priorities of the day. We give our time and attention to the meantime activities until time, resources, and opportunities are aligned.

Passion is motivated by and drives us toward what we desire. For instance, a passion for education can be born through the hope of gaining knowledge, obtaining an academic degree, or educating others. Passion fuels our desire, pushes us through difficult circumstances, and overcomes the temptation to quit. This makes passion vital to the success of every life pursuit. However, reserving passion for things we love to do limits our potential. What if we were passionate about every activity we chose to undertake?

How much more effective could we be if we abandoned the idea that passion is intrinsic, birthed in us through passive means. What if we could manufacture or apprehend passion rather than accepting it as a hunger that arrests us? What if we approached passion as a skill that could be developed through practice and repetition?

Passionate people tend to be very productive. Passion in a marital relationship can be difficult to maintain once life together becomes routine. Healthy marriages thrive not only because couples are passionate about each other. Both husband and wife are also passionate about cultivating a loving relationship. They are not just enthusiastic about whom they have wedded, they are equally passionate about achieving a desired result, marital bliss with the one they love. A common passion oriented towards the marriage union is the glue that produces consistency (and passion) in how couples care for one another.

Resistance awaits every passionate pursuit. In marriage, there will be disagreements. In raising kids, there will be moments of despair. Life sets many traps in the form of financial setbacks, mental blocks, broken hearts, unanticipated losses, disappointments, and the like. Every time we sustain our passion amid adversity, we become more adept at doing so. Therefore, keeping passion alive is the key to success.

Glorify God

Endurance, the ability to push through difficulties or hardships, is often assured for those who tether success to the purpose of their pursuit. This is why the most successful companies put an emphasis on developing a sound purpose statement to motivate their members and employees to unite in a common cause.

We take from Peter's admonishment in 1 Peter 4:11 that the common motivation of all believers for all things is to please God. Thus, being enthusiastic in all we do becomes easier when pleasing God becomes our focus. Whether speaking (in word) or ministering (in deed), the core objective of everything we say and do should have the common intent to glorify God (Colossians 3:2). Paul expands upon this thought in Colossians 3:23 by suggesting that everything we do should be done as though we are doing it for the Lord not a human audience.

God expects each believer to minister as stewards of the gifts He has given. God gives us gifts but challenges us to manage and cultivate them, not for selfish purposes but according to the will and purposes of God. Let those with the gift of language speak the oracles of God and those who serve with the abilities given by Him. When we use our gifts, we honor God in His role as the benefactor and chief beneficiary of the gifts He bestows.

Those who can't be passionate about what they do will likely waste time and energy on things that will result in mediocracy in their hands. They will be better served to leave to someone else the things they don't have the motivation to accomplish. Those who develop the skill of passion have passion for whatever they choose to undertake and do it to the best of their ability.

Be You In Him

We gather from Peter's discourse in 1 Peter 4 that success in ministry and in life hinges on the believer being themselves, being passionate about the person God has called them to be. The desire to mimic the success of others is tempting, but it is almost impossible to reproduce all the factors that went into making us who we are. Although we may share similar gifts, the measure of skill and wisdom in using those gifts invariably differs. We are uniquely made (Psalms 139:14) and uniquely gifted (1 Corinthians 12:4-6) to be successful at being ourselves.

It is important to learn from others, but we should never attempt to become them. Jesus challenged the disciples in Matthew 16:24 saying, "If anyone would come after me, let him deny himself and take up his cross and follow me." Here, Jesus gives a three-fold requirement we must meet to follow him.

First, we must deny ourselves. We must be selfless enough to realize we need him. Following Him requires a conscious decision to forsake our own way and embrace His. Second, we are to take up our cross. He did not ask His disciples or us to bear His cross or the cross of others. Every believer has their own cross to bear. Finally, after denying ourselves and accepting our responsibility, we must walk in His footsteps. We are to mimic God through the example of Christ (Ephesians 5:1).

Mimicking Him helps us become our best selves. However, physically enduring the cross for our sins was His ministry not ours. We mimic Him in the way we walk, talk, and commit ourselves to the will of God. We become more like Him as the Spirit of God empowers us with His character. Jesus does not expect us to be Him; He expects us to be ourselves in Him.

Each believer must passionately take up *their* cross and follow Him, doing God's will His way. In this, we glorify God with our gifts. 1 Peter 4:11 teaches us that the abilities we have, whether speaking or ministering, come from God and are for His glory. Therefore, prudence says that you can only become the best you by taking up *your* cross (*your* role, *your* responsibility, *your* ministry). You only have one life to live, so live yours.

I am reminded of a conflict between Paul and Barnabas over whether they should take Mark with them on their next journey (Acts 15). Paul was eager to visit the churches he and Barnabas met during the first missionary journey. He suggested that he and Barnabas return to see how the churches were progressing. Barnabas offered to take Mark on the journey, but Paul was vehemently against the idea.

Mark left them in Pamphylia and returned to Jerusalem during their last journey. This created a conflict between them. Paul, Barnabas, and Mark were called to be God's servants, but their distinct approaches to ministry introduced considerable friction. The tension between them ultimately ended in each following Christ in separate and distinct ways.

Barnabas saw in Mark what Paul could not and mentored Mark until he became who God gifted him to become. Both Paul and Barnabas were committed to carrying *their* cross, however different. They lived their life based on the purpose and ministry given to them by God. Paul turned out to be a giant in the gospel ministry, writing thirteen books of the Bible. Yet, he later asked Timothy to "get Mark and bring him with you, because he is helpful to me in my ministry" (2 Timothy 4:11). Mark was "now" helpful to him because Barnabas chose to be himself in Christ and mentor the man who would eventually become the writer of The Gospel of Mark.

God is a God of uniformed individuality. We are to be uniformed in regeneration and character but individual in how we express our God-given abilities. Learning from and not repeating the mistakes of others helps us avoid the traps and pitfalls of life. Spiritual and natural advancement can be built upon the failures and success of others, and the lure to reproduce the life of highly "successful" people can be attractive. However, if you only have one life to live, live it like it has never been lived before.

Remember Your Why

The details of life matter but should not become our driving factor. A carpenter excavates the land, lays the foundation, frames the rooms, builds the walls, and then secures the roof. Each step is an important milestone for building a house. Purpose, however, cannot be found in the steps. The carpenter does not excavate the land for the sake of digging holes. The hole, foundation, frame, walls, and roof serve a singular purpose; they are necessary to build the house. When we lose sight of our purpose, our why, life becomes filled with disconnected activities that lead to an arbitrary end. A carpenter who doesn't know he is building a house could very well believe the completed excavation of the ground is the finished product.

It was a cool November morning in Seaside California. The year was 2010. I had just made my way to the track and was gearing up to perform my annual physical fitness test. I dreaded these tests. However, I never failed one during my previous years of active-duty service in the Air Force. This one, however, had me worried.

My exercise regimen since my last fitness test was nowhere near stellar. I could always get max points on pushups and sit-ups. Those I could work on while watching TV or just before bed, but I didn't like running. I never understood those who said that they loved running – I still can't understand it – and it showed in my run-times.

Successfully meeting my goals during the pushup and sit-up assessments did not give me confidence in my ability to pass the overall fitness test. I spent the last year researching and studying for my Doctorate in Meteorology defense, serving as interim pastor for a local church, volunteering as assistant coach of my son's high school basketball team, and staying up late with my newborn baby. I maintained a busy schedule, and exercise was sacrificed on the altar of progress.

I stretched my legs, arms, neck, and ankles and prepared for the race against the clock. My goal was to finish the 1.5-mile run in less than 12 minutes. Twelve minutes would give me enough points to achieve an excellent fitness rating. I never concerned myself with the failure requirements – I never "plan" to fail. I knew success meant running one lap every two minutes.

I felt good once the race began, but things changed quickly. By lap three, the two people in front of me became four, then five, then six, then I lost count. I was distracted by my lungs, which were on fire, and my legs, which developed a painful itch within my muscles. I was in bad shape. As I gasped for air, my mind began to reason with me, "It's ok…just take a break…walk for a bit…you can always retest." It was then that I remembered my "why." I was not running to pass a fitness test.

This run became an assessment of my fitness to serve. Failing the test would be a clear indication that I was not prepared to serve my nation in uniform. Failing would indicate that I was not committed to doing what it takes to support my family. Failing through the lack of preparation would not bring glory to God. My "why" gave me the mental strength to press through the pain and an iron determination to finish the run in less than 12 minutes.

Having a clear and distinct "why" for our actions silences external factors that can otherwise deter, distract, and diminish our efforts. Like the carpenter who understands that the current phase of development does not alter the purpose of the build, the activities we undertake in life are milestones on a journey towards our purpose, to please God.

The desire to please God in everything we do instills within us a resolute strength that becomes evident when we face opposition. In Acts 5:29, Peter and the apostles answered the council and high priest who forbade them to preach the gospel, "We ought to obey God rather than men." No one could deter the apostles from preaching the Gospel because preaching was not the goal. The apostles preached to please God.

We expose ourselves to the undue influence of others when we demote our relationship with God to a secondary aspiration. Jesus, in John 14:42-43, pointed out that there were rulers who believed on Him but did not confess Him because the Pharisees would have put them out of the synagogue. "They loved the praise of men more than the praise of God," He continued. The rulers measured success by their position in society, which deterred them from true success. We relinquish our power to measure success when we rely on others to validate the legitimacy of our actions.

Even in cases where we serve others, pleasing God should define success. Paul encourages us in Ephesians 6:5-6 to serve our human employers from the heart. "Not with eyeservice, as men-pleasers, but as the servants of Christ, doing the will of God from the heart...as to the Lord, and not to men." Herein is the definition of integrity.

We should never allow the presence or absence of viewers to dictate our level of effort.

When we seek to gain the applause of notable men and women, their acknowledgement becomes our reward. Does this mean we do not aim to please others? No. This means we aim to please others when it pleases God. When our actions please God, independent of human judgment and acknowledgement, He rewards us openly (Matthew 6:2-4). Therefore, the primary aspiration, goal, objective of the believer should be to please God in all things.

Figure 2. Remember Your Why

Note: Image generated using Copilot from prompt "black and white image of an excavation for a house in progress." (OpenAI, December 31, 2024)

Chapter 2

TRUST GOD

Defining success is an extremely complicated matter. Early success can motivate us to stay the course and push the limits of our potential. The pride we get from winning and winning early is intoxicating. We are led to believe that we can accomplish, with little effort, what others painstakingly work to achieve. Unfortunately, this type of success can also rob us of the drive that comes with overcoming failure. Success can distract us from pursuing our greatest selves and sometimes our greatest work.

Those who judge success on its own merit will at some point fall victim to its deception. We do our greatest good when we point our passions towards the things we are destined to do. Success, however, can cause us to misalign our efforts with things we enjoy doing but are not essential to our purpose. This is a reoccurring theme among some of the most notable Bible figures.

Joseph's brothers successfully separated him from his doting father, Moses successfully produced water from a rock, Israel celebrated the successful selection of Saul as King, and Jewish leaders successfully orchestrated the death of Jesus. In each instance, they defined success, pursued it, achieved it, and were distracted by it. History characterizes each of these contemporary successes as failures.

In this chapter, we focus on 1 Corinthians 10:1-5 where Paul recalls Israel's salvation, their journey from death to life. We pay particular attention to their escape from Egyptian enslavement (death), their exodus to the wilderness (deliverance), and pursuit of the Promised Land (new life). We will see how they were blessed despite their disobedience, yet they were not allowed to finish the journey they started. What God started with them; He finished without them. Sometimes success is as simple as trusting God when other options appear more palatable, reasonable, and feasible.

GOD'S PRESENCE AND POSITION

> I do not want you to be unaware, brothers, that our forefathers were all under the cloud, and that they all passed through the sea. They were all baptized into Moses in the cloud and in the sea.
>
> 1 Corinthians 10:1-2

Too often we look to the favor and blessings of God as an indicator of our standing with Him. When things go well, we believe we are in His will and that He is pleased with us. It is a grave mistake to use *success* as a gauge for God's approval. Think about it. Is God so binary that He only blesses us when He is proud of us and curses us when we are disobedient? He is far more complex than that. The very gospel of salvation contradicts this notion.

In 1 Peter 18, we see, "For Christ also hath once suffered for sins, the just for the unjust, that He might bring us to God..." Jesus, a just man, was offered for our sins, the unjust. Moreover, the gift of salvation was not earned; none of us are deserving of God's gifts. Salvation is a gift from a gracious God not a proud Father.

Paul's caution in 1 Corinthians 10:1-5 helps those who aim to do God's work understand that they cannot look to the blessings of God as confirmation that they are doing God's will God's way. He reminds the church at Corinth how blessed their forefathers were during their exodus from Egypt. They were led by a cloud and crossed over the Red Sea after escaping the tyranny of Pharaoh, the Egyptian king who held them in bondage for over 200 years. God was their refuge and defense and supplied food and water while they were in the wilderness. He did so because they were His people; not because they were deserving of the blessings they received.

The Cloud Over the Tabernacle

> For the cloud of the LORD was above the tabernacle by day, and fire was over it by night, in the sight of all the house of Israel, throughout all their journeys.
>
> Exodus 40:38

The cloud comforted the children of Israel during the exodus and throughout their journey to the Promised Land. It was a clear and ever-present sign that God was with them. It parked over the tabernacle by day and was replaced by a fire at night (Exodus 40:38). The presence and position of the cloud was informative as to the will of God.

First, the positioning of the cloud over the tabernacle signaled the presence of the Glory of the Lord. His presence invoked both comfort and restraint. I use the word comfort because the Lord was with them but restraint because Moses was not permitted to enter the tabernacle (vv. 34-35).

When God's presence is at work, He fills the tabernacle. Simply put, He leaves no room for us. If we are His tabernacle (1 Corinthians 3:16), being filled with the Spirit means taking comfort in the fact that God is with us. In these rare moments, He leaves no room for our ideas, philosophies, or opinions that contradict His character.

When the disciples were filled with the Spirit on the day of Pentecost in Acts 2:4, it was a unique experience. They were all together with one mind; they were united. It was then that the Spirit enter the room and fill their tabernacle. The filling of their tabernacle resulted in the disciples speaking a language they did not previously know and explaining what they previously did not understand.

The manifested presence of God changed things for the disciples. It instilled a type of boldness that only comes from knowing that God is with you. It must have been comforting to know that God was still with them after seeing the horrific things that happened to Jesus just 50 days earlier, though He appeared several times before His final ascension. However, the Comforter did not come until they restrained and emptied themselves enough for God to fill them with His Spirit.

Second, the positioning of the cloud over the tabernacle dictated their movements. God led Israel's journey Himself. Moses spoke to God on behalf of Israel, bore the shepherd's staff, and gave instructions. However, the people followed the move of God. When the cloud was lifted from the tabernacle, Israel packed their bags and readied themselves for the next leg of their journey to the Promised Land. If the cloud remained, they held their position (vv. 36-37). They only moved when God moved.

It is important to note that verse 38 says, "For the cloud of the LORD was above the tabernacle…in the sight of all the house of Israel, throughout all their journeys." This phrase is significant in that God only spoke to Moses face to face (Deuteronomy 34:10), yet He communicated with "all the house of Israel" through the positioning of the cloud. God directs His leaders but also communicates His movements to all who journey with Him. Although Israel was not allowed to receive God's commandments directly, they were never left to guess whether they were heading in the right direction.

Like the cloud, the presence and position of God in our lives should marshal our movements. Natural and spiritual leaders are responsible for articulating the vision, mission, responsibilities, goals, etc. They even plot the course for the future. Each believer, however, must remain close enough to the tabernacle to see the presence and position of God for themselves.

Israel would not have been able to convince Moses to travel until the cloud was lifted and vice versa. In like manner, when God is present – we are filled with His Spirit – we will always recognize His position. If we do not depend on His presence, we will find ourselves moving when we should be waiting and waiting when we should be moving.

The Cloud at the Sea

> But the children of Israel walked upon dry land in the midst of the sea; and the waters were a wall unto them on their right hand, and on their left.
>
> Exodus 14:29

The cloud was there for Israel to help them through the first major obstacle of their exodus, the Red Sea (Exodus 14:19-30). Pharaoh, the king of Egypt, and his army pursued Israel, pinning them against the sea. They underestimated the presence and position of the cloud in representing the ever-present and all-powerful God.

Exodus 13:18 tells us that Israel left Egypt "equipped for battle." In the next chapter, Exodus 14:10, we see that "they were greatly afraid" at the sight of Pharaoh's pursuing army. The cloud that went before them was a clear indication that God was with them and that He was leading them. Their swords, shields, helmets, pitch forks, etc. did not equip them for battle. The cloud that went before them was their battle ax. Could it be that "they were greatly afraid" because they trusted in their carnal weapons (see 2 Corinthians 10:4).

When the ever-present God is with you, He is more than the whole world against you. Every fear for the believer is irrational. God is faithful and He never fails. When he makes His presence clearly known, follow Him. When His direction isn't clear, stay the course.

Israel followed God right into a trap. They were not skilled enough to fight Pharaoh's army and had no way to escape. There were mountains on both sides and a sea blocked their path. Although they felt helpless, God's presence signified that the enemy's trap was God's plan (Exodus 14:4).

Trials and tribulations are opportunities for God to receive glory. It is at these "Red Sea" moments that His presence shifts from leading to fighting for us. The pillar of cloud adjusted its position and "went from before their face and stood behind them." Israel did not have to use their weapons. God fought for them.

Israel simply needed to stay the course and keep moving forward. The presence of God was still with them as they crossed the Red Sea, but His position changed. At this point they had to trust Him, even though they could not see Him.

There have been times when God has been silent, or I just couldn't hear Him clearly. In those times, I simply stay the course and continue moving forward based on where I believe He is leading me while He works out what I've left in my wake. Fear is never rational for the believer because God is always present regardless of His position.

Maslow postulates, in his hierarchy of needs, that one of the most basic of all human needs is safety. Survival depends on personal security amid environmental and human threats that jeopardize our continued existence. The cloud represented the ever-present God's twenty-four-hour protection. Israel's safety was never in question, and neither is ours.

The exodus of Israel teaches us similar lessons. We can take confidence in our life's journey even when we do not know what lies ahead or what awaits us at our destination – this too is the moral of Abraham's exodus from Ur of the Chaldeans (Genesis 12:1). God is always present, leading, and guiding us during our Red Sea moments. Our success, therefore, hinges on what we do in these moments. Will we sit paralyzed at the bank of the river or press forward allowing God to marshal our movements?

GOD'S PROVISION

> They all ate the same spiritual food and drank the same spiritual drink; for they drank from the spiritual rock that accompanied them, and that rock was Christ.
>
> 1 Corinthians 10: 3-4

Paul shifted from the cloud and sea example of God's benevolence to remind Israel of the meals He provided during their ancestral exodus. God was not only present to guide and defend them with the cloud and sea, but He was also present to provide their most basic needs, food, and water.

The Food

> Then the Lord said to Moses, "Behold, I will rain bread from heaven for you. And the people shall go out and gather a certain quota every day, that I may test them, whether they will walk in My law or not.
>
> Exodus 16:4

Two months after leaving Egypt, Israel grew indifferent towards God's deliverance at the Red Sea. Their memories of Egypt and the trappings thereof made them long for slavery. Born in bondage, they were not conditioned for freedom. Pharaoh was no longer the source of their security and sustenance. Pharaoh provided "pots of meat" and bread (Exodus 16:3). Now, they murmured as though the God who delivered them could not feed them.

Israel's grumblings did not go unnoticed. God provided supernatural food to satisfy their hunger. It was a miracle food, spiritual food, manna from heaven. This gift was a demonstration of God's grace and benevolence. The manna also exemplified the purposeful, always timely, and unparalleled nature of God's gifts.

We should note that our active participation is an essential element of God's blessings. God sent Israel quail in the evening and bread in the morning in response to Israel's complaints because they murmured about missing Egyptian meat and bread (v. 13). They received food from above, but it fell to them to collect and ration it.

As common with God, instructions accompanied His blessing. Not only were instructions common but also necessary. Moses, amid Israel's confusion, explained that the small round things on the ground was bread the Lord provided for them to eat. God can do the impossible, and we should never expect His gifts to conform to our expectations. God makes a habit of surpassing what we ask or think, always exceeding our expectations (Ephesians 3:20). Moses' explanation first helped clarify Israel's understanding of the gift, then he gave them the proper steps necessary to lay hold of the blessing.

Israel was directed to only collect enough bread for the day, except for the sixth day; they were expected to gather a two-day supply. These stipulations served as a daily test of their reliance on God as a reliable provider. If He could set them free, He could surely sustain them.

God's gifts, as with any gift, must be accepted and possessed before it expires. The manna, like dew in the morning, evaporated as the day progressed (v. 21). This gave them a limited time to collect the manna. If they overslept, forgot, or minimized its importance, they would miss their daily blessing. This principle can be applied to salvation.

Salvation is a gift of God that must be accepted and possessed before it expires. God's mercy, like the manna from heaven, is renewed every morning (Lamentations 3:22-23) and expires every day. Each day we live is a gift from God, an opportunity to accept Jesus as savior. Everyone will, however, face the day when His mercy and our time on earth expires. Not accepting the gift of salvation or apprehending it will be inexcusable.

The gifts of God are for a season. Paul even cautions us that the usefulness of prophecy, tongues, and knowledge will expire (1 Corinthians 13:8). The manna did not flow in the Promised Land, only in the wilderness (Exodus 16:34-35). Israel was called to worship God in their own land, and the manna ensured they had the strength to get to the place of promise.

The gifts of God are provided to fortify us for our journey towards our destiny. Those who synchronize themselves with God's timeline and embrace his gifts will be well fed and strengthened to do his will.

The Drink

> Behold, I will stand before you there on the rock in Horeb; and you shall strike the rock, and water will come out of it, that the people may drink."
>
> Exodus 17:6

About 70 percent of the world is covered with water, yet only about 3 percent is drinkable. Humanity's need for water forced early civilizations to concentrate along waterways and near wells. Furthermore, most of the human body is made of 50 to 60 percent water. We can survive much longer without food than water. Israel experienced what we have proven scientifically; water is key to survival.

Israel's trip to the Promised Land was peppered with miracles. God sent ten plagues to convince Pharaoh to release them from slavery. God protected Israel from Pharaoh and his army as they stood trapped at the Red Sea. God divided the Red Sea so Israel could escape Pharaoh's army without so much as getting their feet wet. God ended Pharaoh's tyranny by drowning him and his army as they pursued Israel across the Red Sea. He protected them with a cloud and fed them manna from heaven. Miracle after miracle, God demonstrated His power, protection, and provision during Israel's deliverance.

Israel, in Exodus 15, composed songs to celebrate God's deliverance. They sang, "The Lord is my strength and song, And He has become my salvation." They continued, "Who is like You, O Lord, among the gods?" and concluded, "The Lord shall reign forever and ever." Their joy overflowed as they recounted their Red Sea deliverance. Thirst, however, interrupted their songfest, turning their festive celebration into shared despair.

Moses spent three days in the desert looking for water before finding it at Marah (v. 22). Finally finding water must have brought immense joy to Israel, but their joy was short lived. The water was not drinkable; it was "bitter water" as described in verse 23.

Israel finally found water, but it was an unfinished blessing; the water required sanctification. The bitter water had to be reconditioned for Israel's consumption. Israel found themselves in a dire situation. If they did not find potable water soon, death was certain.

What do you do when you finally obtain the object of your pursuit only to discover that it does not match your expectations? You consumed a significant amount of energy on it. You exhausted resources for it. You spent precious time chasing it. Did you give up, fix it, or complain about it? Israel often chose the latter.

Blaming others for the problems we face can never yield the results we desire. Israel was where God led them. He allowed them to settle in Marah. Only God can right the wrongs of our current state. Moses demonstrates this by calling on God to handle Israel's bitter water blessing.

In this desperate moment, Israel "complained against Moses," and Moses "cried out to the Lord." As Israel complained about their plight, Moses sought God to fix the situation. God instructed Moses to cut a branch from a nearby tree and toss it into the water. Miraculously, the bitter water became sweet.

Israel eventually discovered that their bitter-water blessing was the early stages of God's plan. God grants – those who follow Moses' approach of seeking and trusting Him – the means and methods necessary to transform (sweeten) bitter relationships and situations into thirst quenching and wholly satisfying oases. This was one of many times during their journey that they would look to God to do the impossible.

Israel traveled from one water source to the next. They traveled from Egypt to the Red Sea and from the Red Sea to Marah. Their next stop was Elim. Elim's twelve water wells made it an ideal place to camp. After Elim, they passed through the Wilderness of Sin to camp in Rephidim. Rephidim did not have a source of water (Exodus 17:1).

Camping in a location without water was a problem, and Israel was not shy about voicing it to Moses. They "contended with Moses, and said, 'Give us water that we may drink.'" Their passionate request suggests they were overcome by fear and anger. They ignored God's intervention during previous thirsty moments and chastised Moses for bringing them from Egypt to die in the desert (v. 3). They were extremely distressed and so on edge that Moses became concerned that they were on the verge of stoning him (v. 4).

Water was available at their previous stops, though not potable in Marah, but now they camped further inland and did not have access to a water source. The dry and desolate Wilderness of Sin presented the perfect conditions to reinforce the power of the ever-present God. God was aware of Israel's dependence on water to survive, yet He led them to camp in this inhospitable place. The ever-present God would show them that they did not need an ocean, river, or well to quench their thirst. If He could give them bread without dough, then He could give them water without a well.

God heard Israel's faithless (and frequent) complaint and satisfied it with a miracle; He turned a rock into a fountain. God, as with the manna, gave Moses four specific instruction. He told him to 1) go ahead of the people, 2) take elders, and 3) hit the rock 4) in a familiar place (Exodus 17:5-6). God would produce water from the rock on Mount Horeb, signifying that Israel would never thirst again.

First, Moses was told to go ahead of Israel to Mount Horeb. Mount Horeb was a familiar place. This is the place where God enacted His purpose for Moses (Exodus 3). This is where Moses led his father-in-law's sheep and encountered the burning bush.

Mount Horeb was not new to Moses; he had been here before. Until now, they followed the cloud. Here, however, Moses was entrusted to lead. This trust was not born in the moment; it was cultivated over time. Even those who are called to lead are not prepared to lead until they establish history with God. Great moments do not make leaders. Leaders are made for great moments. Moses knew this place as the Mount of God, and he was now charged to lead Israel into a similar understanding.

Second, God instructed Moses to bring some of the elders with him. Leadership is a lonely venture, but a visionary leader never leads alone. As Israel became more fractured, they turned their anger towards Moses and God. God used this moment to encourage Moses to enlist some help, the same advice Jethro, his father-in-law, would admonish him to do in the very next chapter (Exodus 18:17-23). Moses was caught between God and the people. He could speak to God alone, but he needed the elders, wise and well-respected men, to help keep the fragile group of ex-enslaved together.

Third, God instructed Moses to bring his rod, the rod that turned the Nile River into blood and split the Red Sea. The rod was used in these instances to demonstrate God's destructive power. Now God would use the same rod to manifest His life-giving power.

God instructed Moses to bring something familiar to help him accomplish what had never been done. We saw God use this approach with Moses when He sent him to confront Pharaoh; God showed him what He could do with his rod and sent Aaron, someone familiar, to accompany him.

Familiar situations increase our confidence, and confidence has a way of increasing faith. Our confidence increases our faith by providing a sense of security in unfamiliar circumstances. At other times, familiarity can make us overconfident in our abilities and minimize our reliance on faith.

Moses exhibited overconfidence in his own abilities in Numbers 20. The children of Israel had made it to the desert of Zin and were faced with a similar situation as in the Wilderness of Sin. They camped in a location void of a natural water source. The desert climate, the lack of water, Israel's thirst and grumbling, God's compassion, Moses' rod, and the rock were familiar. This time Moses did not need his rod; God told him to speak to the rock.

Rather than following God's direction, Moses allowed this familiar moment to make him overconfident. Moses was very particular in performing God's commands as directed when he felt he was in over his head. In this instance, however, Moses had been in a desert where there was no water, dealt with the grumblings of the people, and saw water springing forth from a rock. This was not new, it was familiar. Therefore, with great confidence and indignation, he chose not to speak to the rock. He acted based on what he knew worked rather than the Word of God. He hit the rock. In fact, he hit it twice.

God provided water in both instances, when Moses hit to the rock in obedience and disobedience. Although Moses successfully retrieved water from the rock, he was not allowed to enter the promised land. God provided water for the people, but this was not Moses' best moment.   We must fight the temptation of familiar things and situations that can deter us from doing God's work His way.

Figure 3. God is Our Provider

Note: AI, Microsoft Copilot, generated Image using prompt, "black and white image with bread and a water vase." (OpenAI, December 31, 2024)

Chapter 3

PERSEVERE

UNRELENTING PERSISTENCE

Now He who establishes us with you in Christ
and anointed us is God, who also sealed us and
gave us the Spirit in our hearts as a pledge.
2 Corinthians 1:21-22

Israel's exodus is much more than a story about a triumphant God, a blessed people, and a reluctant, yet faithful, leader. Paul opens our eyes to the true nature of the things that took place as they journeyed through the wilderness from Egypt and the Promised Land. He states in 1 Corinthians 10:6, "These things took place as examples to keep us from craving evil things as they did."

Paul maintained, in vv. 7-13, that we should not repeat the sins of Israel nor complain as some of them did. Israel's experience should serve as a warning to us. Israel thought they were doing the "right" thing, but they could not have been more wrong. We are encouraged not to be overconfident but remain cautious. Those who stand firm, as Moses did, are still susceptible to fall. However, God is always present to help us stand when familiar situations tempt us to "smite the rock."

> Wherefore take unto you the whole armor of God, that ye may be able to withstand in the evil day, and having done all, to stand.
> Ephesians 6:13

The call of God is executed from an upright position. It is deftly important to be found either standing or rising. Paul offered the church at Ephesus tools to stand in difficult times (Ephesians 6:13). He introduced them to the armor of God, which he further described in verse 14: the truth, righteousness, the gospel, faith, and the Spirit. The armor presented by Paul is wholly offensive. Each item either protects the front of or is wielded by the soldier. He very subtly suggests, however, that our most powerful weapon and defense is our posture.

Paul encourages us to stand, if only as a last resort. When all else fails, keep standing, he says. Stand for *truth* when lying seems more expedient.

Stand for righteousness, doing the right thing, for the right reason, and in the right way, even when doing so is a disadvantage. Stand for the *gospel* when living for Jesus becomes an offense. Stand in *faith* when doubt assaults the trust we have in God. Stand in the *Spirit* of God when His silence suggest we are standing alone. After you have prayed, fasted, and sought counsel and the word, the most important thing we can do is stand.

Thanks to God, we never have to stand alone. As much as Paul admonishes the church at Ephesus to stand, he acknowledges in Romans 14:4 that whether someone stands or falls should be left to their master. We stand for God and Him alone. Although we are called by God to the benefit of others, He is who we aim to please. We stand in Him and for Him. Therefore, if we combine Ephesians 6:13 and Romans 14:4, we get a greater understanding of what it takes to stand in impossible situations. After doing everything to stand, we can depend on God to hold us up and make us to stand.

Every believer must bear the burden of standing in the face of great trials and temptations. A point that is driven home in the next few verses. Paul pivots to a contemporary Christian controversy to encourage believers to stand firm and unite in the faith that binds us. In a prelude to his instructions on observing the Lord's Supper, which he covers in 1 Corinthians 11, Paul uses the blood and body of Christ to further emphasize the believers' connection with each other as well as the children of Israel.

Those who are called to do God's work are unified through Jesus Christ and share in the promises of Israel. These facts serve as measures against which all actions should be weighed. First, we share in the blood of Christ (v. 16). His blood cleanses us from all unrighteousness. Second, we share in His body, which was broken for us. We are unified in His blood and body. Jesus demonstrated this during His last supper with the apostles.

The book of Matthew, chapter 26, tells us that Jesus, while eating with the disciples, took bread, broke it, gave it to His disciples, and told them to eat it. Paul's message of unity is clearly demonstrated by Christ. Jesus took one loaf of bread and divided it for the disciples and encouraged them to partake in the same bread (v. 26). In a similar manner, He took a cup and encouraged them to drink from it until nothing remained (v. 27). Both the bread and the cup represented His body and blood, respectively.

Paul leaves no room for confusion. The body and blood of Christ are the distinguishing factors of salvation. Salvation through any sacrifice besides Christ is idolatry. Although the followers of Christ are many, we are all unified through His body and blood. The bond we have with one another is forged through the unity we have with Christ. Our fellowship with Christ is the culmination of the communion Israel established by eating the sacrifices made upon the altar of God (v. 18).

Fully Committed

> Since there is one bread, we who are many are one body; for we all partake of the one bread.
> 1 Corinthians 10:17

Can a person be characterized as a "Christian idolater?" The phrase itself is a contradiction. How can those who are one in the body and blood of Jesus also serve idols? It simply isn't possible. We cannot be one with Christ, yet eat, in faith, the bread and cup offered to idols. The unity of the body requires that we resign ourselves to honor the sacrifice of Christ and forsake all others. How can we unify in Christ if we are divided in our commitment?

Jesus said in Matthew 6:24, that we cannot love two masters. We will love one and hate the other, meaning we will inevitably obey one and betray the other. A heart that is divided cannot do God's work His way. The double-minded are not dependable. In fact, 1 Corinthians 10:22 implies that a divided heart "provokes God to jealousy." God's anger is kindled against the double-minded because their loyalty is as steady as the wind, which is not wedded to any particular direction.

James 1:8 tells us that a double minded person is unstable in all their ways. Their judgment is inconsistent; their decisions are unpredictable; and their words are unreliable. The instability of the double-minded is not confined to a single situation; it affects every action they take. It lies at the core of who they are. The indecisiveness of the double-minded signals an inward struggle, principally aggravated by a deficit of wisdom and faith.

In the preceding verses (vv. 5-7), James urged his readers to pursue wisdom and ask God for it by faith. With a phrase intended to motivate and inspire, he encouraged them to seek God who is a liberal giver and reiterated the need to accompany our request with faith. What can we attain from God without it? Faith is the substance of the things we hope for (Hebrews 11:1), but doubt, or wavering, is the enemy of faith. A wavering mind lacks commitment, which puts faith in the balance. We cannot trust God and doubt Him. We cannot pursue Him and run from Him.

James 4:8 says, "Draw nigh to God, and He will draw nigh to you." Every path we take must be vectored in a single direction, towards God. In so doing, we pursue His righteousness. As we draw closer to God, He transforms our hearts, minds, and deeds. Our hands and hearts are cleansed, and our faith is made whole. Only a purified heart can cure a double mind.

A "Christian idolater" is an abnormality that cannot exist. God expects us to put our faith solely in Him with absolute confidence. Those unified by the body and blood of Jesus Christ are unified in their faith in God. However, this unity is disrupted by faith that waivers and is corrupted by idol worship.

Paul acknowledges that idols are false gods (v.19) yet cautioned not to participate or give credence to their observances (v. 20-21). God is not jealous of idols, but His jealousy is provoked when we worship them. Sacrifices made to idols are not tainted in and of themselves. The sacrifices are as pure as they were prior to the sacrificial rites of idolatry. Paul's concern is the spiritual impact on the believer's faith. We cannot worship demonic forces and expect God to be pleased or even apathetic towards such things. Those who engage in God's work are not authorized to participate in ceremonies or rites that celebrate other god(s). Our worship is reserved for Jehovah through Jesus Christ.

SACRIFICE OF LIBERTY

All things are lawful for me, but all things are not expedient: all things are lawful for me, but all things edify not.

1 Corinthians 10: 23

After Paul established the disagreeable nature of idol worship, he approached eating food offered to idols from a different perspective. He introduced this new approach in verse twenty-one and summarized it in verse twenty-three above. The grace of God is so extensive that it overshadows all laws that stand against us. The grace of God affords the believer liberty to do anything that does not carry with it an offense to God or others. At face value, this grace-born liberty would appear to expand the scope of what we can and can't do. However, further examination of Paul's application reveals the opposite (v. 23-30).

Liberty can be a liability

Although we have liberty, we must always consider how our actions will affect others, believers and unbelievers. Those who aim to do God's work must understand and accept the requisite sacrifice, a sacrifice that is non-negotiable. We are asked to place ourselves on the altar, sacrificing our will for His. In doing so, our grace-born liberty is placed on the sacrificial altar. Is this not the story of Abraham?

God promised and provided Abraham a son, yet commanded that Isaac, his son, to be his mountain-top sacrifice. Genesis 22:2 says that Abraham loved Isaac. Sacrificing Isaac was not a small task. Isaac, the son Abraham prayed for, received, and now cherished, would be sacrificed on an altar for the glory of God. We know, as he lifted his hand to complete the sacrifice, God set him free from the obligation.

We have this great mandate of sacrifice in common with Abraham. Our liberty is the gift God expects us to put on the altar. He does not call for the death of our children. He beckons for us to surrender our will. Romans 12:1 says it this way, "I beseech ye brethren, by the mercies of God, that ye present your bodies a living sacrifice, holy, acceptable unto God, *which is* your reasonable service."

Abraham denied himself his love for Isaac and went to the altar to not only sacrifice his son but his liberty as well. Abraham did not complete the sacrifice of his son, but the sacrifice of his liberty was clear and complete. Abraham's obedience culminated when he cast the sacrifice of his liberty on the altar as a condition of worship. When we offer our will, our liberty, to God, we do so as living sacrifices conditioned for worship.

The day of rest, the sabbath, is also the day of worship. Leviticus 16:31 describes it as "a sabbath of rest unto you, and ye shall afflict your souls, by a statute forever." The New International Version of the Bible replaces "afflict your souls" with a more modern phrase, "deny yourselves." Israel sanctified, or set aside, the sabbath as a holy day unto God. Similarly, denying oneself, or setting aside fleshly impulses, consecrates our hearts towards righteousness. Self-sacrifice was and is a necessary condition for proper sabbath observance. What better way is there to honor God with our gifts than to glorify Him with ourselves?

Jesus, in Matthew 16:24, told His disciples, "If any man will come after me, let him deny himself, and take up his cross, and follow me." Following Christ does not come without sacrifice; discipleship demands it. The true power of God's grace working in us is demonstrated in our ability to walk in liberty and our willingness to sacrifice it when necessary.

When we sacrifice our liberty, we condition and incline our hearts towards God and the service of others. Paul, in our primary text, calls for believers to be disciplined enough to deny themselves what grace has given them free access. Such sacrifices become essential when our grace-born liberty becomes a liability. Our liberty becomes a liability when it works counter to the work and will of God.

True followers of Christ are expected to put the will of God and good of others above themselves (v. 24). At the very least, do as Jesus admonished the scribe who inquired about the first commandment. Jesus said we should love God and love our neighbor as we love ourselves (Mark 12:31). Salvation delivers us from the power, penalty, and presence of sin (2 Corinthians 1:10); and God, through salvation, delivers us to assist in the deliverance of others. Jesus was obedient to God in that He sacrificed His personal desires to die for the world. He did not allow His liberty to become a liability in fulfilling God's will. The believer must be prepared to make the necessary sacrifice when the liberty afforded by grace causes others to stumble.

Liberty for All

Paul summarized 1 Corinthians 10 in verses 31-33 by offering three definitive reasons believers should rise to meet each moment with a willingness to deny themselves. Everything we do should 1) bring glory to God, 2) not work to impede an unbeliever's pathway to Christ, and 3) not inhibit Christian growth. Those who answer the call to do God's work cannot go wrong if they set these as their guiding principles.

God's chief concern in this world, as expressed in 1 Timothy 2:4, is that "all men be saved." Timothy begins the chapter by exhorting the saints to pray for all men. Specifically, he calls for supplications (prayers for specific needs), prayers (general prayers), and intercessions (petition for God's will), and giving thanks (prayers of gratitude) for all men. Each prayer is distinct and has its own objective. However, each prayer is offered with the same purpose, that all men be saved.

At its core, God's work is not about us. He calls upon us to sacrifice what He has freely given us so that others may benefit. As Paul states in 1 Corinthians 10:33, "I'm not seeking my own good, but the good of many, that they may be saved." Selfish intents must be forsaken. When we yield ourselves to become Christ's example on earth for believers and non-believers, we open ourselves to be used by God to accomplish things that reach beyond our sphere of influence and limited lifespan.

Paul, in 1 Corinthians 10, discussed the eating of bread and drinking of the cup of idols as a gateway to promote the central truth of the gospel. His discourse was not about eating and drinking. It was about serving God and others. Whether people were eating or drinking the correct things was essentially a distraction. Unfortunately, these types of distractions persist with every generation. Should we cut our hair, should we wear pants, should we play instruments, should we dance, should we speak in tongues, and the list goes on. Paul teaches us that we have been liberated from meat and drink, and now they serve as distractions, diverting our attention from the mandates of God's work, serving God and others.

God's work is bigger than us; thus, our success is His success. He trusts us to do the things that bring Him glory, persuade non-believers to repent, and draw believers closer to Christ. The believer must war against the temptations of idol worship, contemporary distractions, and our grace-born liberty that can pull us away from God's work.

Chapter 4

FOCUS

Success in every endeavor is contingent upon one's ability to focus on the task at hand. Failure to accomplish goals or objectives can be a consequence of many things, but it most often results from a lack of proper focus – not just an inability to stay focused but also choosing to focus on the wrong things. The ability to maintain a proper focus is a constant struggle. The archives of history hold many tales of deception, devastation, and disobedience, which were ushered in when the iron gates of concentration were left open.

Time and time again, major biblical figures changed the tides of time by averting their attention or focusing on the wrong thing at the most critical moments. Eve, the mother of all mankind, turned her heart from God's word and focused on the forbidden fruit. Jonah turned his heart from God and focused on his own desire to see the destruction of the city of Nineveh. David turned his heart from his men who were fighting for his kingdom and focused on the wife of one of his soldiers, Bathsheba. Judas turned his heart from our savior and focused on 30 pieces of silver. Of course, in every aforementioned case, the focus shifted towards things that satisfied the desire for selfish gain.

We should be careful, however, not to dismiss all distractions. Some are useful in adjusting and realigning our focus. Abraham, while sacrificing his son, was distracted by a ram caught in the thickets. Moses, while tending to his father-in-law's sheep, was distracted by a burning bush that would not be consumed. Jesus, while traveling to resurrect Jairus' young daughter, was distracted by a woman with a blood disorder. Peter, while traveling to Gaza, was distracted by an Ethiopian man reading from the book of Isaiah. Distractions can work for or against the will of God. It can be difficult, but not impossible, to determine when the realignment of our focus has righteous merit or sent as a device of the enemy.

In this chapter, we look to 1 Peter 4 to obtain the tools necessary to overcome the distractions that arrest and steal our attention away from God's will and work. Four focus areas are evident within the text. The believer who set out to do God's work must maintain an inward, Godward, and onward focus, which helps avoid the temptation of an outward focus where we concentrate on the shortcomings of others.

INWARD FOCUS

1 Forasmuch then as Christ hath suffered for us in the flesh, arm yourselves likewise with the same mind: for he that hath suffered in the flesh hath ceased from sin;

1 Peter 4:1

After studying 1 Corinthians 10, we understand that the willingness to sacrifice our will for God's glory and His people is an essential part of our faith. It is a war we must fight and win. Our human desire for self-preservation will not sacrifice what is dear to us, yield what is rightfully ours, or put aside sin without a struggle.

The believer must always begin God's work with an honest look in the mirror. A mirror only reflects the image before it. If we stand in front of it with a mask, makeup that covers our scars, or dye that changes our hair color, we will see an image we created not the person we are. It takes courage to strip away the filters of self-confidence, pride, holiness, wisdom, and honesty we use to hide our true selves from others.

The believer who looks at themselves squarely in the mirror, without disguise or concealment, will discover that they themselves are God's first work. With an inward focus, we begin the process of gaining power over our weaknesses, never allowing ourselves to be manipulated because of them nor tormented by them.

Expect Opposition

> I find then a law, that, when I would do good,
> evil is present with me.
>
> Romans 7:21

Paul, in Romans 7, looked in a symbolic mirror and saw a war within himself. Earthly desires and impulses stood in opposition to his spiritual transformation. Paul's struggle is as common as the sunrise. Although his heart's intent was to please God, his mind was known to stray off course, providing alternatives and weak justifications for protecting the status quo.

Paul, in Romans 7:14, declares that "the law is spiritual: but I am carnal, sold under sin." The laws, edicts, and commands are righteous and incorruptible. They are holy in their expression, execution, and aims. God's plans are only flawed by their dependence on humanity's ability and willingness to convey and perform them. This makes the enemy within us the greatest threat to God's will and work.

As God has determined to allow the wheat and the tare to "grow together until the harvest" (Matthew 13:30), believers must embrace their new life in Christ knowing that there is a traitor in the midst. The carnal (natural, fleshly, selfish) mind stands against God; it does not embrace the laws of God because it cannot do so (Romans 8:7). The carnal mind promotes sleep when the spirit says pray. It touts consumerism when the spirit encourages benevolence. It craves freedom when the spirit urges surrender. The carnal mind is ever present, working to impede our progress.

Paul concluded the chapter with a question, "…Who shall deliver me from this death?" (Romans 7:24), then gave us the answer to the question, God through Jesus Christ. He noted that the struggle will continue. His transformed mind will continue to war against his carnal mind. Although Paul tells us in the next chapter that we are not condemned nor powerless to combat the enemy within us, this will not relieve us from the persistent struggle and suffering our carnal mind fosters.

Suffering is Winning

> That he would grant you, according to the riches of his glory, to be strengthened with might by his Spirit in the inner man;
>
> Ephesians 3:16

Peter encourages us in 1 Peter 4:1 to have the same mind as Christ. He reminds us that Christ suffered in the flesh, and we should do the same. He concludes the scripture with an empowering proclamation. He said, "he that hath suffered in the flesh hath ceased from sin." In this, he suggested that those who suffer, or deny themselves, have victory over sin; the very act of suffering wins the battle.

The context of the scripture leads us to conclude that Peter is not referring to the physical suffering Christ endured on the cross. Rather, it points to His temptations and struggle against sin. Per the writer of Hebrews 4:15, Jesus was in all points tempted like us but never sinned. Peter is encouraging us to have the same resolve, to fight and win the inward struggle. In so doing, He gave us the solution to Paul's war against the flesh. By denying ourselves, we subdue the lust of men and submit to the will of God (v. 2).

The Bible does not identify a specific incident where Christ suffered from within, but the gospel writings are dependable sources to uncover the lessons Jesus taught. His most notable temptation came in the wilderness (Matthew 4:1-11). This was one of the most prominently known places where Jesus struggled in the flesh. Before He put forth His hands to commence God's work, He allowed His inward resolve to be tested. Satan tempted Him to 1) break His fast, 2) prove Himself and 3) forsake His God.

Although He was tempted with external things, each temptation was designed to win the battle of wills. The word was His weapon, and the struggle secured His victory. From Peter's perspective, His refusal to yield to the devil's temptations evidenced a victorious struggle.

First, Satan appealed to the lust of the flesh and suggested Jesus turn rocks to bread. Jesus was hungry after fasting 40 days, which made the temptation ordinary and necessary. It was just him, he could have complied, eaten the bread, and no one would have known. Yet, he refused Satan's nudging saying, "Man shall not live by bread alone."

Second, Satan pushed for a pride-of-life response by challenging who Jesus was, His capabilities, and who He could become. The devil urged Jesus to prove that He was the Son of God by casting Himself down and commanding angels to save Him. Jesus, in a weakened state from fasting, was faced with a decision many have faced when doing the work of God. Do I prove what I know to be true?

Pride rises when our self-confidence is confronted. Pride is never satisfied with knowing our own worth – who we are, what we can do, and what we can achieve. It seeks to justify our confidence through tangible proof(s). This holds true whether the doubt we contend with originates from others or ourselves. When challenged, there is a strong urge to prove what cannot be naturally seen. Pride pushes us to plant and reap out of season. Those who follow Jesus' example will rely on the word to win the battle within.

Jesus, as with the previous temptation, relied on the word of God to win the battle within and rose victorious. He did not yield to the desire to prove He was the Son of God, as Satan suggested. He refused to prove His Sonship to Satan because He knew the His Father would prove it at a time chosen best suited to His will. He was destined to perform miracles that *would* prove (not *to* prove) He was the Son of God. He raised the dead, proving (not *to* prove) He is the giver of life. He walked on water, proving (not *to* prove) He was omnipotent. His works spoke for Him. Jesus won the internal battle against pride, proving that He possessed true self-confidence in who He was, His abilities, and what He was sent to do.

Third, Satan sought to distract Jesus by appealing to humanity's natural lust of the eyes. Solomon in Ecclesiastes 2:10 stated that he was a great man in Jerusalem, "And whatsoever [his] eyes desired [he] kept not from them…" He concluded this discourse in verse 11 with his discovery that it all was vanity and vexation of spirit. The eyes are deceptive. They depreciate the value of our possessions and feed an insatiable appetite for what appears attainable.

Our investment in what we see can become an idol we can never satisfy. We can give our resources toward building something noteworthy, our energy towards achieving something great, or our mind towards discovering something significant. We can invest our all in the things we desire, even in the name of God, but these things cannot love us nor save us. Selfish desires can only divert our focus from the work and will of God.

Jesus journeyed to the mountain to pray and fast. Now, at the end of his fast, Satan arrives to show Him how he could improve His current living conditions. He offered Jesus the kingdoms of the world and their riches if Jesus would worship him in return. This, another distraction, called for a sacrifice that was not worth the reward. God's work is its own reward.

Jesus did not come to rule natural kingdoms; He came to setup an eternal kingdom. The short-sighted aims of Satan were not consistent with His long-term goals – things that appeal to the lust of the eyes usually aren't. Therefore, Jesus declared that we only worship and serve God. We do not worship Him because He satisfies the ravenous appetite of our eyes. We worship Him because He is God and worthy of our adoration.

Jesus, in each temptation, depended on the Word of God to win the inward battle against the desires of His flesh, pride, and eyes. Though He rose victorious, the victory was won with an inward focus. The words He uttered were spoken by a victorious Savior. Even if He never said a word, the victory was already won. His words were the evidence of the victory achieved by His inner man.

Jesus refused fleshly desires, rejected prideful urges, and resisted visual lures. He denied His flesh and showed us that refusing to do what our flesh presses us to do is winning. Our victory is won before it is revealed. Jesus exited His period of temptation victorious, not because of His actions but because of His decisions.

Godward Focus

2 That he no longer should live the rest of his time in the flesh to the lusts of men, but to the will of God.

1 Peter 4:2

In Matthew 4, we observed Jesus securing victory over Satan during His wilderness experience. His victory was not won through miracles, powers, and wonders; it was won from within, demonstrating the importance of having a strong faith and appreciation for God's word. Peter (1 Peter 4:1) characterized Jesus' experience as suffering in the flesh. In the next verse, Peter announces that suffering in the flesh leads to a life focused on God's will.

Believers who deny themselves and suffer for Christ are liberated from the dictates of sin and the flesh. We experience a spiritual release, enabling us to focus on God's work and will. With a commitment to looking squarely into the mirror, accepting what we see, and placing ourselves on the altar, we increase our capacity to recognize and embrace our God and His will.

Live Unto Him

> For I through the law am dead to the law, that I might live unto God. I am crucified with Christ: nevertheless I live; yet not I, but Christ liveth in me: and the life which I now live in the flesh I live by the faith of the Son of God, who loved me, and gave himself for me.
>
> Galatians 2:19-20

Prior to the saving work of Christ, the law served as Israel's conduit to God. God gave Israel laws to teach them how to serve Him as well as each other. His instructions were designed to create a people who were sacrificial in their actions, disciplined in their thoughts, and caring in their hearts. God's righteousness was articulated in the law, and Israel was expected to live according to every word. Of course, this was not possible as explained by Paul in Romans 8:3.

The weakness of the law was its reliance on mankind to perform it. The law exposed our sinful nature and highlighted our shortcomings. The law could not justify or sanctify. In the court of life, the law served as a prosecutor, and we stood accused, seeking justification without a defender. However, God sent "His own Son," Paul continues in Romans 8:4, "in the likeness of sinful flesh, and for sin, condemned sin in the flesh."

Jesus broke the yoke of sin and condemnation of the law. Rather than living to fulfill the law, we now live unto God, to please Him. Our relationship begins and ends with Him. We know and understand His word, walking in it and honoring Him because of it. We do not strive to love God and one another because there is a price to pay if we fall short. We follow Jesus even in this. Paul stated in Romans 6:10, "[Christ] died unto sin once: but in that he liveth, he liveth, unto God."

Our focus should be on God, understood here as the Father, Son, and Holy Spirit. The Father planned our salvation, Jesus purchased it, and the Holy Spirit sealed it. As they worked to bring about salvation, they are working together to sustain it.

The Father guides our lives according to His plan to bring us to an expected end (Jeremiah 29:11); the Son advocates for us with the Father (1 John 2:1); and the Spirit teaches and comforts us (John 15:26). While these roles are distinct, they are not mutually exclusive. We should not assume to fully understand God using simple categorizations. These generalizations are useful, however, as we seek to understand His role in the life of the believer.

We are admonished in Hebrews 12:1-2 to lay aside every weight, the things that hamper us, "looking unto Jesus the author and finisher of our faith." We must set aside the things that weigh us down or keep us up at night. The scripture encourages us to avert our gaze from the problems and difficulties that stand in our way and cast our focus on Jesus, on the things that bring God glory.

The double-minded believer cannot expect to see what is envisioned when distracted by the weights that hinder, deter, and obstruct their progress. A weight-ward focus – focusing on the weights of the world – is a wayward focus, which does not work towards Godly results. Therefore, the believer must adjust their mind's eye, shifting from a weight-ward focus to a Godward focus, looking to the Father for His plan, Jesus for His forgiveness, and the Holy Spirit for His instruction.

A Godward focus is a unifying force. When we look to God, we are unified in Him. Each believer's individuality compliments another. We speak in many tongues and dialects but with one voice. Our Godward focus synchronizes our ministries, gifts, and talents. Although we walk different paths, we all travel to the same destination. By looking to God, we arm ourselves with the passion of Christ who said in John 6:40, "For I came down from heaven, not to do mine own will, but the will of him that sent me." Those who shift their hearts and minds towards God put their hands towards work that pursues His will.

Live to His Will

> For it is God which worketh in you both to will and to do of *his* good pleasure.
>
> Philippians 2:13

A Godward focus invariably leads to a revelation of His will. Let's take another look at Jesus' wilderness temptations. More specifically, let's consider how God prepared Him for the experience. God is deliberate and intentional in everything He does, and He did not allow Jesus to face His tempter without preparation.

Matthew 4:1 states, "Jesus [was] led up of the Spirit into the wilderness to be tempted of the devil." Jesus did not go to the wilderness of His own accord; He was led there. The Spirit led Him into the wilderness for the express purpose of being tempted by the devil. This happened immediately after the

Spirit descended upon Jesus, after John baptized Him in the Jordan (Matthew 3:16). Jesus did not begin God's work until the Holy Spirit was in place to communicate and clarify God's will.

The believer who looks to God allows the Holy Spirit to be their guide. Paul wrote in Philippians 2:13, that God works in us [through the Holy Spirit and His word] to do His will and do what pleases Him. Jesus called Him the Spirit of truth as recorded in John 16:13.

> Howbeit when he, the Spirit of truth, is come, he will guide you into all truth: for he shall not speak of himself; but whatsoever he shall hear, that shall he speak: and he will shew you things to come.
>
> John 16:13

The Spirit serves as a chaperone for the Godward-focused believer, supervising and prompting us to live to the will of God. Jesus enjoyed the benefit of our God-sent chaperone during His wilderness experience. He overcame temptation by speaking of the Father (Matthew 4:4, 7, 11), and He preached the coming of the Kingdom of Heaven as His first post-temptation action (Matthew 4:17). Both speaking of the Father and showing things to come evidenced the work of the

Holy Spirit. The Spirit speaks of the Father and not about Himself, and He shows us things to come (John 16:13). He tells us what the Father says and what He plans to do.

Jesus repeatedly demonstrated a strong commitment to the will of God. On one occasion, after His disciples returned from the market, they urged Him to eat the food they procured. He refused and said to them, "My meat is to do the will of him that sent me, and to finish his work" (John 4:34). While they were shopping, He met and ministered to a woman at Jacob's well. His disciples were so focused on natural things that they missed the significance of the crowd gathering to validate the claims of the woman who testified of Jesus after meeting Him at the well.

Jesus was intent on living to the will of God not from moment to moment but until it was finished. What a commitment. He was led by the Spirit at every instance. He knew His purpose and pursued it. His battle with His flesh was as common as ours, yet He maintained an unyielding devotion to the will of God. Even as He faced a certain death on the cross, He remained steadfast. His flesh, desiring a more favorable path to our freedom, interrupted His prayer and asked to be relieved of the burden. His Spirit said, "Nevertheless, not my will but thine be done" (Luke 22:42) and lived to the will of God until His final breath, proclaiming, "It is finished" in John 19:30.

ONWARD FOCUS

> For the time past of our life may suffice us to have wrought the will of the Gentiles, when we walked in lasciviousness, lusts, excess of wine, revellings, banquetings, and abominable idolatries: Wherein they think it strange that ye run not with them to the same excess of riot, speaking evil of you:
>
> 1 Peter 4: 3-4

Regret is perhaps the most common element of the human experience. Everyone has experienced moments of loss, aggravated by missed opportunities, mistakes, and misconduct. Recent regrets tend to torment us the most. On the other hand, long-lived regrets that are viewed from a proper perspective can become a trusted navigator, guiding us away from danger and towards a brighter future.

Regret, as with all things, can work for or against us; it can be helpful or harmful. Recent regrets can be paralyzing or compelling. Either way regret is convincing. Regret restrains us, encourages us to limit ourselves in an attempt to avoid future remorse. It can also compel us to heighten our focus and increase our resolve to live a life without regrets.

Verses three and four of 1 Peter 4 highlights the misdeeds that Christians share. We take note that Peter speaks of these deeds in the past tense. Rather than encouraging us to forget the deeds of the past, he encourages us to remember them. We are not defined by our past deeds; we remember them to remind us of who we have become. The emphasis is not on what we did in the *past* but on our *present* habits and associations.

The thoughts of disappointment that keep us up at night and seize our attention during the day can work for or against us. Regret can disrupt our focus, forcing us to relive cancerous moments we cannot cure or sharpen our focus to ensure the mistakes of the past remain in the past.

Leave The Past In The Past

> Brethren, I count not myself to have apprehended: but this one thing I do, forgetting those things which are behind, and reaching forth unto those things which are before,
>
> Philippians 3:13

As much as the Bible is the living word of God, it is also a book of historic events. The wisest among us have given us quotes to appreciate the value of history. William Shakespeare gave us in The Tempest, "The past is prologue" and George Santayana said in The Life of Reason, "Those who do not remember the past are condemned to repeat it." History is extremely valuable in that it informs the decisions that affect our future. This makes keeping the past in the past difficult if not impossible.

Paul, in Philippians 3:13, again lets us see inside his personal struggle. He was convinced that he was not what he desired to be in Christ. Although he progressed from producing Christian martyrs, to growing Christian disciples, he confessed that he was not perfect. Even so, he did not allow his crimes against Christ, his period of greatest regret, to hinder his progress.

Paul determined to forget the things that were behind him and press for the things before him. He did not use the term "forget" to suggest that he erased his past from his memory. His history was his testimony, which he often used to declare Christ as savior (Acts 26:9-11). We therefore look at the term "forget" in a different light. By implication, Paul suggested that he "neglects" the things that are behind; he did not give his past power over his present nor his future. His admonition to forget the past was not a function of memory but of focus.

Jesus, on one of His trips to Jerusalem, encountered "a great multitude of impotent folk, of blind, halt, withered, waiting for the moving of the water" at Bethesda, a pool at the sheep market (John 5). People gathered at the pool in hopes of receiving relief from their ailments. They simply had to be the first person in the pool after the angel "troubled the water," which happened seasonally. Jesus seeing the multitude singled out a man that was lame for thirty-eight years.

We are not told how many healing seasons the man experienced at the pool, but his situation was dire. His infirmity rendered him helpless. A lame man could never be expected to win the race to the pool; someone would have to help him if he were ever going to be the first one in. The years of disappointment must have been more debilitating than his physical condition.

Perhaps, in a crowd filled with excitement and hope, this man's deep despair and misery stood out. Jesus asked him a simple question, "Wilt thou be made whole?" The obvious answer was "yes." He, like the rest of the multitude, came to the pool to be made whole. Rather than answering the question directly, he complained about his past, diverting attention away from his current condition. Thankfully, Jesus had an iron focus, ignoring the man's past and addressed his present state. Ignoring the man's complaint, He said, "Rise, take up your bed, and walk."

The Future is Sown Today

The importance of focusing on the future is made clear by Philippians 3:13. We should remember and understand history but refuse to give it life. Progress comes when we reach for the future – when we pursue it, hope for it, live for it. Reliving the past, our regrettable moments, complicates the present and poisons the future. Those who focus on past events cannot fully appreciate the grace and mercies of the present nor foresee the impacts of changing times. A rearward focus will invariably cause us to miss the signs that announce the sowing season for future progress.

Jesus was a master of using historical events to calibrate present events and add context for future events. In every case, He focused on today. John 8 records an instance where spiritual leaders brought a woman caught in adultery and asked Him if she should be stoned. He said, "He that is without sin cast the first stone," imploring each person to calibrate their actions relative to their own history. Their history was invoked to arouse the sentiment of grace, not guilt. Being convicted by their own history, her accusers left one by one.

The story does not end with the men walking away, it ends with Jesus' recommendation for the future. We do not know the circumstances nor motivation for her adultery, but we are given the context of her future. Jesus moved from her past and focused on how her present impacted her future.

Although she was caught in adultery, the crowd could not condemn her and neither did He. After acknowledging her present freedom, Jesus encouraged her not to repeat the sins of the past. Grace gave her the opportunity to move on. Her future would depend on her ability to start from now with an understanding that her future depended on the decision she made at that present moment.

This is a reoccurring lesson in the biblical text. Peter's story is a particularly interesting case study for embracing an onward focus. Jesus told Peter in Matthew 26:34 that Peter would deny Him three times before the morning. Rather than focusing on Peter's limitations, Jesus invested in Peter's potential. Matthew 26:35-36 tells us that Peter was among the three disciples Jesus chose to accompany Him in prayer. What an iron focus? Jesus' words can be interpreted (not translated), "Peter, you will deny me three times before it's all over...now let's go pray...the future still depends on you."

Peter answered the call in The Book of Acts. He, with extreme confidence, preached what can be heralded as the church's inaugural sermon. The sermon points to the historical record to explain their present reality. He surfed the waves of history pointing to the words of Joel, the acts of Jesus, and the testimony of David to proclaim Jesus as "both Lord and Christ." Peter did not mention his own history of success and failure – he previously denied Christ. He moved on from the past and focused on the 3000 souls that said yes to the saving power of Jesus Christ that day.

The People Problem

One of the difficulties in leaving the past behind is the people that tether us to it. People are notorious for digging up and bringing to light the deeds we have discarded. They push us towards paths that are contrary to our destiny and inconsistent with our new character.

We should be careful here to clarify that sin is the problem not people. There is nothing more important to God than people. In fact, Christ died to save all people from sin's corruption. Yet, sin remains to corrupt the actions of those who reject His cure. Lust, a self-serving desire that is never satisfied, lies at the core of sin. It always preferences personal progress, even at the expense of others.

Peter reminded his readers in verse 4 that the unconverted witnesses of their past could not relate to their present. They considered the believers "strange" and were spitefully critical of them for conducting themselves differently. The text models a situation where people that were married to the past despised the progress of those who left them behind. We cannot help but wonder if the believer's regeneration served as a source of conviction for those who had yet to embrace their grace-born liberty.

This type of situation plants the believer between two temporal realities. On the one hand, the new man basks in God's saving grace and hope for a Christ-centered future. The old man, on the other hand, is tempted to return to the deeds of the past. Under the advisement or ridicule of the ambassadors of our past, we are encouraged to abandon our purpose and discard our destiny. The believer must decide whether to move onward or backward.

The believer who aspires to fulfil their purpose must move on from the past, maintaining an inward, Godward, and an onward focus. The believer who allows people to become their purpose will naturally focus on the desires and expectations of people. Every believer should have a passion for people; after all, salvation and spiritual growth of people is the supreme objective of the believer's ministry. However, those who see people as their purpose are more inclined to move backwards rather than onward.

Jonah focused on the sins of Nineveh and lost sight of his purpose to relay God's message (Jonah 1-4). He disagreed with God's intended grace towards Nineveh. When God told him to preach repentance to Nineveh, he refused. By focusing on the people of Nineveh, he abandoned the will of God. It took a raging storm and a belly of a fish experience for him to realign his focus, concluding in Jonah 2:9, "…I will pay *that* that I have vowed. Salvation is of the Lord."

Abraham, after years of failed attempts to have a son, yielded to the compassion of his barren wife, Sarah. Sarah suggested he abandon his faith in God for a son to conceive a child with Hagar (Genesis 16-17). Abraham succumbed to the pressure of Sarah, and had a son with Hagar, Ishmael. Even though God disapproved the union, He honored

Abraham's love for his son and promised to bless Ishmael.

Abraham and Sarah's doubt led to a misaligned focus, causing them to abandon the purpose God established in His irrevocable covenant to make him a great nation. God reaffirmed His promise and affirmed that His covenant would be established with the son of Abraham and Sarah and that Isaac's place as the son of promise was non-negotiable. Despite Abram and Sarah's detour, God allowed them to move onward as promised.

Peter lost focus in the most critical moments in history. As Jesus suffered contractions of new life, suffering abuse ahead of his labore on the cross to birth Christianity, Peter focused on what people thought of him (Matthew 14:66-72). When pressed whether he knew Jesus, He denied it, not just once but three times. One of the accusers suggested that he spoke like Jesus, so "he began to curse and to swear, saying, 'I know not this man of whom ye speak.'" Jesus prophesied that Peter would deny Him three times before the rooster crowed twice, and right on cue, Peter slid back into his old ways.

An onward focus overcomes distractions and backward-oriented people pressure. We saw Jesus, earlier in this chapter, heal a lame man at the pool of Bethesda (John 5). He gave his attention to one man among so many who gathered at the pool. He could have healed them all, but Jesus left the pool through the multitude of people even before the lame man could get His name (John 5:13). He did not go to Jerusalem to heal the multitude; He purposed to preach the work of the Father and the Son to save humanity.

People define success for themselves as well as others based on personal goals and objectives, and we tend to focus on the things we deem important. When our God-given purpose becomes our priority, our passion for other things, which may be important, become secondary. The believer must remain vigilant to overcome the prompting of well-meaning people that advise us to deviate from our purpose because our God-given purpose extends beyond our sphere of influence, temporal limitations, and finite understanding.

Those who understand purpose will respond like Agabus and Paul's company (Acts 21), "When he would not be persuaded [not to go to Jerusalem], we ceased, saying, 'The will of the Lord be done.'" People are not the believer's purpose, yet the believer cannot fulfill his or her purpose without a passion for people. After all, every purpose bestowed by God is hewn with a passion for humankind.

Chapter 5

CULTIVATE YOUR GIFTS

But watch thou in all things, endure afflictions,
do the work of an evangelist, make full proof of
thy ministry.

2 Timothy 4:5

Most begin life with gifts that are soon taken for granted. As an infant, we learn that our eyes are gifted with sight, our ears with hearing, our tongue with language, our feet with balance, and our hands with the ability to grasp. The more we put these gifts into practice the more fluent we become in using them. Some elect to advance these gifts and become experts at reading body language, listening for what is not said, speaking many languages, performing circus-like feats of amazing balance, or crafting masterpieces of art and masonry. These individuals surface the true potential of their abilities by not allowing their gifts and talents to remain idle. We must, as Paul told Timothy in 2 Timothy 1:8, "stir up the gift of God, which is in [us]" by exercising them.

The gifts of God can be spiritual or natural. Spiritual gifts are given primarily to affect growth in the believer and saving faith in those living without Christ. Like natural gifts, spiritual gifts can be cultivated to increase their effectiveness. We offer our natural gifts and talents to contribute to the furtherance of God's Kingdom, but spiritual gifts are used in ministry (service) as God dictates and affords opportunity.

THE ONTOLOGY OF SPIRITUAL GIFTS

But the manifestation of the Spirit is given to every man to profit withal.
1 Corinthians 12:7

Ontology is a philosophical study of the nature of things or beings. The word originates from the Greek terms ontos (to be) and logos (study of), the study of being. This definition, however narrow, provides sufficient framework for our discussion. Ontologism proposes that there are two philosophical means of confirming truth. In our context, the existence of God is a "necessary truth" or a "contingent truth."

Figure 4. The Ontology of God

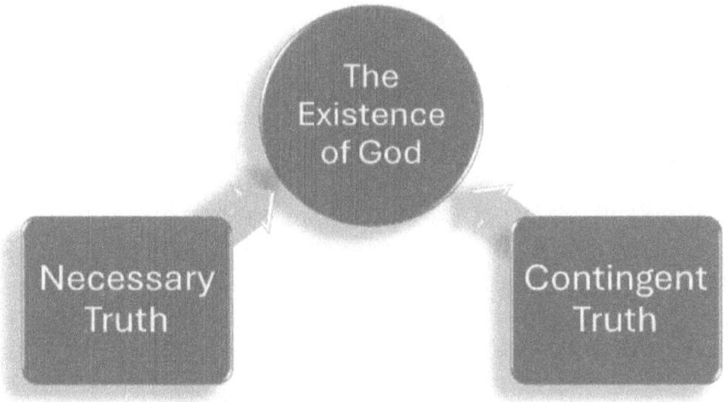

Note: Ontologism proposes that there are two philosophical means of confirming God's existence, necessary and contingent truth.

Necessary Truth

Necessary truth argues that God must exist independent of human experiences. The fact that God created all things is at the core of Christian faith, which makes His existence a necessary truth. We learn in Acts 17:28 that "In him, we live, and move, and have our being." The scripture continues by quoting contemporary poets, "We are His offsprings," contending that we are born of God and cannot exist unless He exists.

In nature, things that are orderly are expected to be arranged by someone or something. Who would happen upon a shelf filled with books in alphabetical order and conclude the books were placed at random? Who would come across a beaver's dam in the forest and surmise that the neat, vertically stacked sticks resulted from water flowing within the open stream? Who would discover a bird's nest resting in a tree or on a mountain and conclude that the wind consolidated the brush in a round concave fashion? The surprising thing about our world is most things that appear to be chaotic are governed by the laws of physics and can be mathematically modeled.

Our existence hinges on the perfect anatomical balance of our universe, planet, and body. Human existence depends on the sun providing the perfect amount of energy from a perfect distance, the earth being the perfect source of food, the atmosphere providing the perfect environmental range of pressure and oxygen; and the human body, with all its flaws, being complex enough to adjust to seasonal changes and injury. It is impractical to believe that the natural state of the world is inclined towards order rather than chaos. Thus, the improbability of our existence is evidence of God's existence.

In like manner, the resurrection of Christ is a necessary truth. The Christian faith unravels without it. Paul points out that our preaching and faith are useless if Christ was not raised from the dead (1 Corinthians 15:14). We become false witnesses of God without the resurrection. Our grace-born salvation and hope of resurrection become invalid. Therefore, to be a follower of Christ, one must hold to the fact that Adam brought death by sin to mankind, and Jesus brought the hope of resurrection by the grace of God (Roman 5:12-15).

Contingent Truth

Contingent truth asserts that God's existence is proven through human experiences. Christian faith maintains that Jesus is God, and He is the Messiah who was sent from God. How then can we associate the Christian faith with "contingent truth" when the existence of God stands as truth whether we believe it or not? This dichotomy is a source of cognitive dissonance – an uncomfortable feeling arising from two contradictory truths.

How can belief in God be contingent on or born through human experiences? Jesus exemplified this idea when He told His contemporaries to examine His works (the miracles performed, the wisdom wielded, and prophecies fulfilled) to find proof of God in Him (John 10:37-38).

Although effective, this method is not flawless. Contingent truth depends on private interpretation of personal experiences. Jesus warns in Matthew 24:24 not to rely solely on signs and wonders because they can also be performed by false Christs and prophets. Furthermore, Jesus performed miracles, yet some didn't believe He was the Messiah.

Thomas, one of Jesus' disciples, stated that he would not believe in the resurrection of Jesus, as described by the other disciples. He required a personal experience with the resurrected Christ before he would believe (John 20:24-25). In the verses that follow, Jesus did in fact return and encouraged Thomas to touch his wounds; "be not faithless but believing." Thomas then believed. Although Jesus did not use our terms *contingent* and *necessary* truth, we detect them in His response to Thomas' faith in verse 29:

<u>Contingent Truth:</u>
"Thomas, because thou hast seen me,
thou hast believed:"

<u>Necessary Truth</u>
"...blessed are they that have not seen
and yet have believed."

It is far better to accept the existence of God as a necessary truth; however, belief for some is contingent on their experiences and how they interpret those experiences. Our propensity towards contingent truth undergirds the need for Spiritual gifts. As we saw with Thomas, walking by faith (i.e., trusting God) and not by sight (i.e., trusting our experiences) (2 Corinthians 5:7) can be one of the most difficult challenges a believer or unbeliever will face.

Everyone has a different threshold of belief. Like pain, we differ in how much we can tolerate. Some relent as the slightest discomfort, and some believe with minimal impetus – they have child-like faith. God knows our threshold of belief and provides tailored experiences that are necessary to activate our faith.

In the book of Acts chapter two, the disciples spoke in various tongues (languages), and over 3000 people were converted to the Christian faith. This miracle, along with a sermon by Peter, a disciple of Christ, was enough to activate the faith of those who heard the disciples speak clearly in their own language. It is not disclosed whether any of these people knew Jesus, heard Him speak, or witnessed the miracles He performed. What is clear, however, is hearing His disciples master their dialect overnight made Christ a necessary truth. They did not experience the gift themselves. Their interpretation of the Gift given to the disciples led to only one conclusion, Peter was telling the truth about Jesus.

Herein lies the highest purpose of our gifts: to activate and increase the faith of unbelievers and believers, respectively. God gives us gifts to help each other as we journey towards our destiny. This cannot be overstated. Understanding the significance of our gifts (and talents) is to understand our role in unlocking the power of God that works through us to change hearts and minds.

When speaking of spiritual gifts, Ephesians 4:1-12 often comes to mind. Here, we are told that we all receive grace in measure (v. 7). Each person receives grace that is sufficient for their deficiencies (2 Corinthians 12:9), and God supplies additional grace as required (Romans 5:20). God's general gift (grace) is then followed by specific gifts.

"Everyone of us is given grace" and like a warrior that returns from battle with the spoils of victory, Jesus returned from the grave, ascending in omnipotence and immortality. He set captives free and gave gifts unto man. He freed us from sin and death and distributed spiritual gifts, equipping us for the work of the ministry. The gift of grace is but the first of many gifts our God and savior graciously gives to believers as evidence of His existence.

THE AIMS OF OFFICIARY GIFTS

Paul, in Ephesians 4, named five specific, officiary gifts (apostles, prophets, evangelists, pastors, and teachers), which appear to designate positions rather than spiritual skills. The unique skill of a gifted apostle is proselytizing, a gifted prophet is prophesying, a gifted evangelist is evangelizing, of a gifted pastor is shepherding, and a gifted teacher is teaching. So, Paul may have found it useful in this instance to categorize the gifted by what they are gifted to do.

Figure 5. Aims of Officiary Gifts

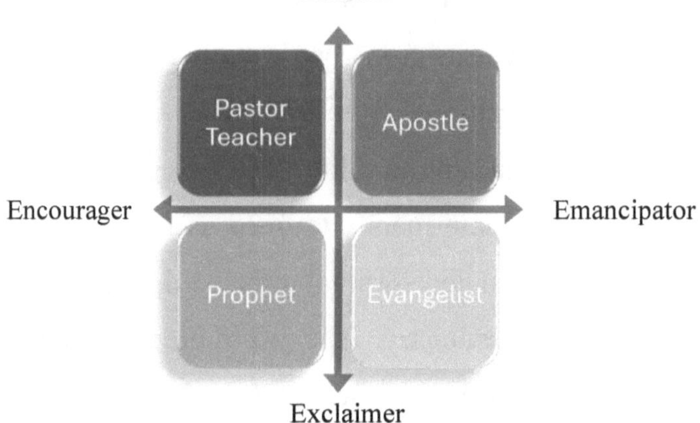

Note: All believers can operate in every spiritual gift, but God has given specific officiary gifts to the church to perform primary roles in edifying the body of Chirst.

Contextually, Paul referred to those endowed with spiritual gifts as gifts themselves. As outlined in Ephesians 4:12, spiritual gifts and their bearers are given to the body of Christ for at least three purposes. They are given for the perfecting of the saints, the work of the ministry, and the edifying of the body of Christ. From Figure 5, we infer an additional purpose, to spread the gospel. Note that those who bear the gifts are not listed as intended beneficiaries of the gifts. These gifts are not given for the pleasure of the gifted but to empower believers to educate, emancipate, and encourage the body of Christ and exclaim God's word.

Perfecting the Saints: Educate

God gifts some believers with the aptitude to elevate Christian knowledge and understanding. Pastors and teachers, for example, are given wisdom to instruct believers in the ways and will of Christ. Christian growth depends on sound doctrine and a clear understanding of God's word. Gifts are given so believers can go from unwitting children to astute followers of Christ (vv. 14-16).

Working the Ministry: Emancipate

Gifts are given first for spiritual growth and second for church growth. By church growth, we mean numerical, not local but universal church growth. God gifts the church with apostles, prophets, evangelists, and pastors and teachers to prepare the church to do the work of the ministry (Ephesians 4:11). It is worth noting that the gift of teaching is not exclusively a pastoral gift (1 Corinthians 12:28). The work of the ministry is reconciling souls to Christ, compelling and converting unbelievers. The work of the ministry unifies believers and gifts toward a common cause. Paul encourages pastors by way of his letter to Timothy to do the work of an evangelist, make full proof of his ministry (2 Timothy 4:5). As believers progress toward perfection, gifts are employed to increase the knowledge and understanding of each member of the body, preparing them for the work of the ministry.

Edifying the Body of Christ: Encourage

Finally, Paul states that gifts are given for the edifying of the body of Christ, the act of building up believers. Although third in the list, Christian edification is no less important. Prayer, faith, love, forgiveness, compassion, benevolence, psalms, songs, etc. all work to encourage the believer as we await Christ's return. The gifts of God work together to cultivate Christian unity, comfort, hope, and faith.

Speaking God's Word: Exclaim

Spiritual gifts are critical in the advancement of salvation. Hebrews 2:3 reminds us that our salvation is the escape route from the destruction of sin. It was born through Jesus Christ and perpetuated by those who speak His words. Even further, the next verse says, "God also bearing [witness to our salvation], both with signs and wonders, and with divers miracles, and gifts of the Holy Ghost, according to his own will." Gifts are like the fruit of a fertile tree, signaling to its beholders that it is alive and healthy.

COVET THE BEST GIFTS

Paul listed gifts in 1 Corinthians 12 suggesting that perhaps some gifts are more important than others. Some may view this text as Paul's list of prioritized gifts where the more important gifts were mentioned first, and the rest were named in a descending order of precedence. Those who hold this view may find support in verse 31 where Paul says, "covet earnestly the best gifts."

In truth, this interpretation goes against the scriptural context of Paul's perspective on gifts. Paul spent most of the chapter espousing unity through God's gifts. Each gift is given by one Spirit for the profit of all (v. 7). God gifts each member of the body as it pleases Him (v. 18). Every gift is necessary (vv. 19-22), even the ones we consider inferior (v. 23). In fact, God assigns greater honor to the less prominent gifts to combat the rise of division within the body (vv. 24-25).

Paul builds his argument on this foundation; all gifts (and the gifted) are special and have a specific purpose. Although we may esteem one gift above another, God does not use the same delineation. Gifts are not given to be worn as an ornament of distinction among believers but a catalyst for unity within the body of Christ.

Historical Precedence

Why would Paul spend the chapter arguing that every gift is as important as the next only to conclude that some gifts are more important than others? It appears more likely that Paul's enumeration of the gifts in verses 28-31 is not a prioritized list. He is most likely pointing to a historical precedence of spiritual gifts cascading from Christ's resurrection to the establishment of the local church.

Figure 6. Spiritual Gift Given to the Church

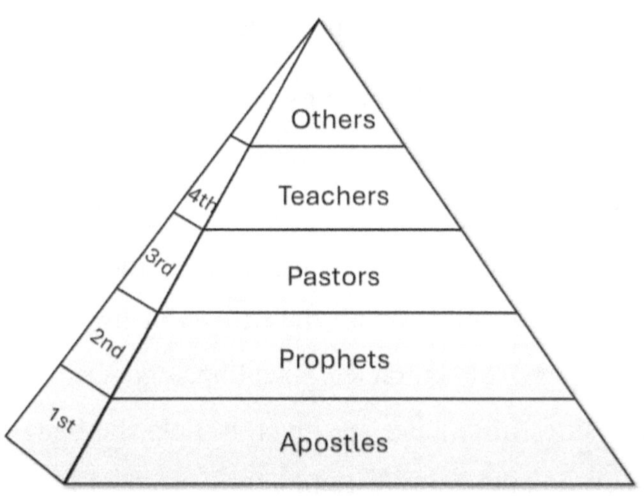

Note: Paul enumerated the gifts not in order of presidence but the order which they entered the body of Christ.

First, there were apostles, the disciples who were prophets, teachers, miracle workers, and healers.   These apostles were responsible for spreading the gospel to all nations compelling humanity to accept the saving knowledge of Christ. Second, He gifted prophets to build upon the foundation laid by the apostles, proclaiming Christ and His promises, challenging new believers, and converting unbelievers. Thirdly, He gifted pastors to lead and comfort believers.   Fourthly, He gifted teachers, along with pastors, to gather and instruct converted believers, elevating their knowledge and understanding of the gospel of Jesus Christ.

Paul listed apostles who introduced the gospel, prophets who proclaimed the gospel, and pastors and teachers who explained the gospel. After which, he shifted his focus to gifts that are not normally associated with the offices of the church. The gifts of miracles, healing, governments, diversities of tongues are given to help the body of Christ function as intended.

Gifted for Unity

Again, the numbering of the gifts appears to be less about the intrinsic value of the gift and more about their order of entry in the development of the body of Christ. With this view of verses 28-31, we discover a consistent call for unity. Are all apostles, prophets, teachers, workers of miracles, healers, speak in tongues, or interpret, Paul asked rhetorically. He previously established that each member is unique and uniquely gifted. At the end of the chapter, he advised that if they insisted on coveting gifts, they should seek to master the best gifts and revealed the greatest gift (love) in chapter 13 followed by prophecy in chapter 14.

1 Corinthians 12 tells us that God distributes gifts and sets them in the church. He mentions a short list of gifts – the list is not exhaustive – to make the point that each gift (member) is important. The gifted should therefore strive to know and understand the purpose of their gift, for with each gift "there are differences of administration [ministries] and diversities of operations [effects]" as Paul stated in 1 Corinthians 12:5-6.

Paul spent the entire chapter of 1 Corinthians 13 arguing the supremacy of love and its place above all other spiritual gifts. Then, he followed the love chapter with a chapter dedicated to prophecy (to speak under the inspiration of God), suggesting prophecy is a gift worth coveting (1 Corinthians 14:39). By examining how Paul presented prophecy and tongues, we gain a practical approach to assessing the purpose of our gifts.

Spiritual gifts can benefit unbelievers as well as edify believers. "He that speaketh in an unknown tongue," Paul said, "speaketh not unto men, but unto God," and because no one understands him, only the speaker is edified (v. 2). Thus, prophecy is a more productive gift in church gatherings, Paul argues, because the gift of prophecy is not given for the unbeliever but the believer (v. 22), yet prophecy can also convert unbelievers into sincere worshipers of God (vv. 24-25).

Paul did not contrast unknown tongues and prophecy to diminish the importance of speaking in an unknown tongue. Rather, he sought to ensure the gifted were purposeful in how they used their spiritual gifts. He did not consider the gift of unknown tongues to be useless within the body of Christ. Unknown tongues only became problematic when they were used as a stand-alone gift in public worship.

Paul made four statements that discredit the notion that he opposed or saw no merit in the gift of unknown tongues. First, Paul spoke in unknown tongues more than his readers (v. 18). Second, tongues serve as a sign or evidence to unbelievers that the power is from God (v. 22). Third, the gift of tongues should be paired with the gift of interpretation of tongues (vv. 27-28). Finally, do not forbid anyone from speaking in tongues, Paul cautioned (v. 39). Every spiritual gift was vital, even speaking in unknown tongues.

The value of the gift is measured in how the gifted employs these special skills. Paul considered prophecy more effective than unknown tongues in a church or group setting. However, prophecy spoken in an empty room cannot seed the fruit of edification, exhortation, or comfort for others. Unknown tongues, on the other hand, would be well suited for such unaccompanied moments where believers pray and fellowship with God. Paul used prophecy and tongues to accentuate his aspiration for a unified church. He could have used other examples to present his case, but the discontent engendered by those who spoke in unknown tongues during corporate worship provided a useful context for the discussion.

Like prophecy and tongues, each gift has its ideal context and application. Paul concludes chapter 14 with a statement that encapsulates the meaning of his discourse. "Let all things be done decently and in order," he said in verse 40. All things (every gift) must be used properly (in an honorable manner) and in order (as appointed by God).

Gifted for Reconciliation

> Every good gift and every perfect gift is from above, and cometh down from the Father of lights, with whom is no variableness, neither shadow of turning.
>
> James 1: 17

God does not choose qualified people to work for Him; He qualifies and gifts believers to accomplish His will. The gifts of God are uniquely tailored to each believer, based on what God has equipped the believer to do within this present age. Furthermore, these gifts of the Spirit are a revelation of God's power working in us. The gifts differ, as Paul says in Romans 12:6, "according to the grace that is given to us." God's gifts are not earned; they are freely distributed.

Apostles James, Peter, and Paul espoused gifts as an important aspect of Christian service. James espoused that the power of Christ delivers believers from sin and death, and that all good and perfect gifts come from God (James 1:15-17), and we can become doers not just hearers of His word through Jesus and His grace. Without grace, our sins cannot be forgiven, and reconciliation is not possible without forgiveness. This naturally makes the gift of grace the center of gravity around which all other gifts orbit.

> As every man [believer] hath received the gift, even so minister the same one to another, as good stewards of the manifold grace of God.
> 1 Peter 4:10

Peter encouraged gifted believers to share their ministerial gifts, hospitality in particular, with one another (1 Peter 4:9-10). We are not only recipients of God's grace; we are to be "good stewards of the manifold grace of God." Peter's word choice suggests that the gifted believer does not own God's gifts. Both natural and spiritual gifts are gifts of grace, and the good steward who renders gifted service ministers God's grace.

Paul speaks of the gift of grace, salvation, and the Holy spirit in each of his epistles but put special emphasis on spiritual gifts when writing to the Corinthians, Ephesians, and Romans. As we explore Paul's writings, let's be careful not to limit the gifts of God to those Paul identified. Although Paul espoused an exact list of officiary gifts given to the church – we hold this to be true because the gifts in Ephesians 4 were given in the context of the resurrection and for the express purpose of guiding and governing the church – God distributes gifts as needed to assist us in fulfilling His will and our purpose.

Paul, in 1 Corinthians 12:7-12, gives nine examples of spiritual gifts, highlighting that these ontological gifts (gifts that point to the existence of God) come from God. These gifts evidence God's existence, which is necessary for the advancement of the Great Commission (Matthew 28:18-20).

These nine ontological gifts can be grouped into four categories: Cognitive, Transformative, Perceptive, and Linguistic. Each gift is marked by a common characteristic and goal. They are a manifestation of the Spirit of God through us for the good of others (v. 7). Let's explore them in turn.

Figure 7. Ontological Gifts

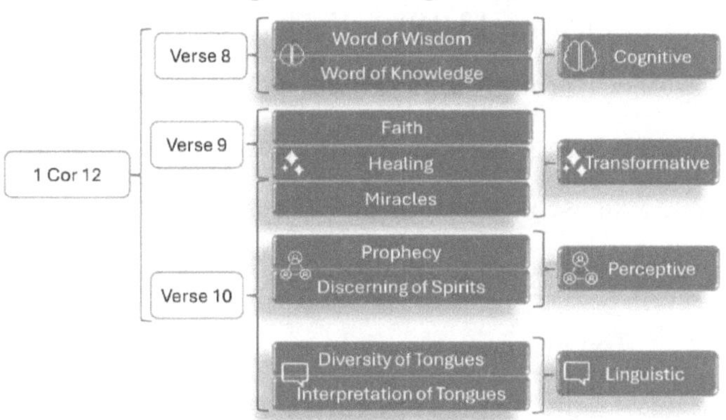

Note: 1 Corinthians 12:1-8 outlines the four categories of gifts that work as evidence of God's existence..

Cognitive Gifts

> Let no man deceive himself. If any man among you seemeth to be wise in this world, let him become a fool, that he may be wise.
>
> 1 Corinthians 3:18

Cognitive gifts that come from the Lord include wisdom, understanding, and knowledge. Spiritual *wisdom* naturally understands without knowledge, *understanding* naturally comprehends what is known, and *knowledge* naturally retains what is revealed.

How do we gain wisdom? Can you lose it or transfer it? Paul tells us, "Worldly wisdom is foolishness to God." Therefore, to be wise, we must first become fools to the wisdom of the world (1 Corinthians 3:18-19). Wisdom cannot be taught or gained through experience; you can't age into it. Wisdom is exclusively a gift from God. Therefore, those who seek wisdom can ask and receive it from God who bestows it generously (James 1:5).

Experiences are only as good as the lessons we learn from them. A negative experience can force us to act irrationally or misread opportunities when conditions of our current situation reflect those which previously led to an undesirable outcome. Wisdom, on the other hand, seems to always arrive at the right conclusion, even when the facts are limited, or the best path points contrary to the historical precedent.

People with the gift of understanding possess an extraordinary, cognitive ability to quickly grasp or comprehend new concepts and ideas. Our level of understanding (of people, literature, the world around us) depends on the depth of the reservoir of knowledge from which we draw. The more knowledge we gain, the better we understand. Knowledge, however, does not equal comprehension. By dissecting, connecting, and processing knowledge in new and ingenious ways, the gift of understanding expedites comprehension and thereby abbreviates the learning process.

We've all heard it, "Knowledge is Power!" The cognitive ability to retain and recall information is extremely powerful. Those who are perceived to be knowledgeable are awarded the power of influence. We have a natural tendency to trust people who can speak intelligently in our area of interest. The more the salesman knows about the car on the showroom floor, the more confident we become in their recommendations. A person with a photographic memory can recall facts that others may take hours or even days to commit to memory. Knowledge is the foundation upon which understanding is built and accounts for the information wisdom overlooks.

Transformative Gifts

Jesus and His disciples, while traveling to and from Jerusalem, encountered a fig tree in full bloom yet without fruit. Jesus, being hungry and dissatisfied with the tree's production, cursed the tree. The next day, Peter mentioned to Jesus, with what appears to be amazement, that the fig tree withered away. Jesus replied, "Have faith in God" – His words are perhaps better translated, "Have the faith of God" – and explained that faith doesn't have to be grand to do great things. Faith can be as small as a mustard seed (Mark 11:20-24) and still move mountains.

Those gifted with faith, healing, and miracles are God's instruments to bring restoration and reformation to the human condition. These gifts manifest and demonstrate God's power. Hence, some categorize them as "power gifts." We find it useful to term them "transformative gifts," gifts used by God to alter our physical reality.

Paul's ordering of these transformative gifts (faith, healing, and miracles) lends itself to interesting, ontological implications. The gift of faith is an extraordinary confidence in God. Healing (by faith) supplies the healed (as well as the gifted) with a reliable truth that God exists. Miracles (performed by faith) satisfy the contingent truth required of the masses who are privileged to witness the incredible event.

Believers endowed with transformative gifts exemplify an inspirational confidence in God. Acts 5:12-16, recounts the impact of miracles performed by the apostles in Jerusalem. The constituents of the city demonstrated amazing faith in the apostle's abilities. With unrestrained faith, they laid the sick in the streets in hopes that Peter's shadow would fall upon them as he passed. The transformative power of the Apostles' ministry of faith, healing, and miracles stirred up the faith of those who they encountered, and men and women by the multitudes become believers in Jesus.

Perceptive Gifts

The Gospels often picture Jesus preaching and teaching to multitudes. Matthew 13:1-6 is one of those instances. At this moment, we witness Him sharing a parable of "a sewer that went forth to sew" seeds. Jesus used this short story to emphasize the importance of not just hearing but also understanding the word.

His disciples undoubtedly considered this method of teaching, using parables, to be rather strange. They asked Him to explain the reason He spoke in such a roundabout way (v. 10). In response, Jesus reflected on Isaiah 6:9 to introduce the concept of spiritual discernment. Using the Greek word horáō, (to perceive) in verse 14, He explained that everyone who saw Him and heard His words were not gifted to see beyond (spiritually) what they saw (physically) nor understand (spiritually) what they heard (literally).

Jesus also used the word horáō in verses 16 and 17 when He told His disciple that their eyes and ears were blessed because they could see and hear, respectively. Others could not see nor hear beyond their physical context, but His disciples were gifted to perceive what they saw and heard.

> For verily I say unto you, that many prophets and righteous men have desired to see those things which ye see, and have not seen them; and to hear those things which ye hear, and have not heard them.
>
> Matthew 13:17

Perceptive gifts afford believers the unique opportunity to see what God sees. These gifts, as with the disciples' gift to see and hear, endow believers with a special ability to clearly understand what they see and hear. Everyone has what we call intuition. However, intuition is not always correct.

We sometimes misjudge situations, outcomes, and people. Perceptive gifts like prophecy and discerning of spirits are not limited by our experiences or expectations but are a manifestation of the Spirit of God who hears and sees with perfect accuracy and precision.

Linguistic Gifts

According to the World Atlas of Languages, the world actively communicates in over 7000 spoken or signed languages. Language is central to communication. Without common vernacular, the transfer of knowledge and ideas becomes impossible. God used the division of language in Genesis 11:1-9 to confuse the people of Shinar who purposed to build a city and a tower that would impress the world. God, in response to their pride and ambition, diversified their language to thwart their plans and disperse them. In contrast, the Holy Spirit used the gift of [diversity of] tongues in Acts 2 to bridge the communication gaps that would otherwise limit the spread of the gospel of Jesus.

The gift of tongues or language tears down the barriers of communication. Paul suggests that the gift of tongues can be manifested in heavenly or earthly languages that are spontaneously learned. We discover in Romans 8:26 that when we don't know how or what to pray, the Spirit translates our incoherent thoughts and intercedes for us with unspeakable words. Paul gives context to this in 2 Corinthians 12:1-4 where he recounts the testimony of a man who experienced a vision of paradise and heard "inexpressible things," words the human tongue cannot or should not articulate.

The endowment of tongues and Peter's preaching at Pentecost (Acts 2:1-41), shows us two miracles. First, the gifts of tongues drew a multitude of the Jews together. Second, the gift of tongues empowered the disciples to speak in a manner and dialect that the multitude could understand. People will gather to hear the Word of God, yet what profit is it to the hearer if they cannot understand what is being said?

The people were not "amazed" that the disciples could "speak with other tongues;" they were amazed "because that every man heard them speak in his own language." The gift of tongues is not provided to the body of Christ as a magic trick or feat of amazement. It was not given to solidify the Holy Ghost's presence in the life of the believer. Although, the Jews were amazed and the Holy Ghost's presence was evident, these were not the purpose of tongues.

We must be careful how we establish the doctrine of the Holy Ghost based on Acts 2. If we conclude that the evidence of the filling of the Holy Ghost must come with the speaking of tongues, then we must by necessity also conclude that there must be "a sound from a mighty wind." God is not limited to doing things one way. God empowered the disciples with supernatural power to minister Jesus to "devout men out of every nation under heaven." What better way to spread the gospel than to convert and commission visitors to carry the gospel back to their hometowns?

This event demonstrates the power of tongues and its role in converting "about three thousand souls who gladly received the word and repented." The disciples spoke of the "wonderful works of God" in the language of various places and diverse people, to include Jews (v. 10). The fact that the disciples also spoke under the power of the Holy

Ghost in their own native language is often overlooked.

The miracles of tongues can be demonstrated in the supernatural ability to spread the gospel to those who are not fluent in a common language. However, the gift can also be prevalent in an environment where the gifted speaks in a language native to both the speaker and the audience.

> But when they deliver you up, take no thought how or what ye shall speak: for it shall be given you in that same hour what ye shall speak. For it is not ye that speak, but the Spirit of your Father which speaketh in you.
>
> Matthew 10:19-20

Jesus encouraged His disciples not to think about what they would say when they were detained and questioned about their faith because the Holy Spirit would speak through them. Luke recounts an occasion when Paul requested to speak to a rambunctious mob in Jerusalem who wished him dead. When Paul began to speak, the crowd paused to listen to him because he spoke in their Hebrew language (Acts 22:2). By the time he finished speaking (v. 22), the mob determined to have him killed. Speaking in unknown tongues has the power to impress, but speaking in known tongues, influenced by the Holy Spirit, is both captivating and provocative.

The true power of the event in Acts 2, where the disciples spoke in unknown tongues, is in the fact that those who listened to them heard them in their native language. The sensational display of the gift can sometimes overshadow its true power and purpose. Is it more important that the disciples spoke in languages that the multitude were not familiar with or those who heard them understood them clearly? I suggest the latter. The gift of tongues is "poured out" to magnify God and spread the gospel.

The apostles preached the gospel with varying results. As Peter preached the gospel of Jesus Christ in Caesarea (Act 10:34-46), he was interrupted by the Holy Ghost who "fell on all them which heard the word." They spoke with tongues and magnified God, even the Gentiles, those of non-Jewish descent. Luke took great care to ensure his readers understood the subtext of this event. The intervention of the Holy Ghost and the Gentile's acceptance of the gospel of Jesus Christ serves as a clear sign that Jesus came not just to save the Jews but all who will profess and believe in His lordship.

Paul, in Acts 19:1-7, took a trip through Ephesus where he encountered disciples of John the Baptist. Paul extended to them the full gospel, explaining that John's message espoused that they believe in Jesus. Paul's sermon was not as elaborate as Peter's but just as effective. He clarified John's role as a placeholder until the gospel of Christ Jesus was fully established.

Hearing this, the followers of John chose to be "baptized in the name of the Lord Jesus." Unlike Peter's experience above where the Spirit fell on the Gentiles, and then they were baptized, these believers were baptized, and then "the Holy Ghost came on them, and they spoke with tongues and prophesied" when Paul laid his hands on them (NKJV).

There are three biblical examples where the Holy Ghost manifested Himself with the gift of tongues. In the first recorded instance, the gift was poured out on the apostles, and devout Jews believed. In the second, the Holy Spirit fell on and extended salvation to the Gentiles. Finally, followers of John, who walked in incomplete truth, became followers of Christ Jesus who is the fullness of truth. In all three cases, salvation was the intended result for those who received the gospel message.

We must remain flexible and sensitive to how God desires to use our gifts. We infer from Luke's account that the devout Jews who heard Peter's sermon *were baptized* (Acts 2:41) but did not speak with tongues, the Gentiles at Caesarea spoke with tongues *before they were baptized*, and the followers of John spoke with tongues *after being baptized* unto Christ. The commonality of the instances lies in their acceptance of Christ Jesus and baptism, not the gift of tongues.

In every case, the gift of tongues came after the gospel was spoken and understood. Even the disciple received the Holy Ghost on Pentecost after receiving the gospel from the most gifted orator ever known, Jesus. Sensationalizing the gift of tongues as a hyper spiritual gift overlooks its inherent power to draw sinners to Christ. In 1 Corinthians 14, Paul emphasized the importance of speaking in tongues, not to fascinate but communicate with hearers.

The gifts of God can have many functions, but there's no higher purpose than reconciling souls to Christ. Cognitive gifts work to close the gap between the known and uncertain things in life. Jesus demonstrated the power of transformative gifts to draw huge crowds. Perceptive gifts can minimize the risk of perilous times. Linguistic gifts have the power to escort believers to the grandest stages in the world. The greatest power of these gifts, however, is their ontological argument for the existence of God.

GIFTED FOR REMEDIATION

4 For as we have many members in one body, and all members have not the same office: so, we, being many are one body in Christ, and every one members one of another.

Romans 12:4-5

As one body in Christ (Romans 12:4), each believer can serve a particular role. Although it is possible to possess multiple gifts, the gifts we possess can serve as indicators of our role(s) in ministry. The ministry we are called to perform within the body of Christ is uniquely designed to remedy the disparity between who we currently are and the good and acceptable and perfect will of God for us (Romans 12:2).

"Having then gifts differing according to the grace that is given to us," Paul continues in Romans 12:5, we exercise our gifts according to our faith and in the right season. Thus, the gifted must account for aptitude as well as timing. As the mouth, feet, and hands only speak, walk, or grasp when they are called upon, so it is with the gifts of God. Those who teach, minister, or exhort must wait until God calls upon their gifts and ministry.

As much as Romans 12 is about gifts and ministry, the chapter's central theme is the unity of the body, and we are warned about the power of spiritual gifts to divide us. The gifts are not innately divisive; however, they are entrusted to corruptible vessels who can misjudge their value. The uniqueness of an individual's gift can lead to the false conclusion that one person is more important than the next. The believer's gifts are not merit-based and cannot be earned. Therefore, only God who gifts believers has just cause to boast.

All spiritual gifts flow from the same Spirit, making the resident gifts equal in importance to the development of the body of Christ. The expressed power of spiritual gifts, however, is governed by the completeness of the believer's surrender to God's endowment (2 Corinthians 12:9-10). As each member of the body operates in their respective ministry, the body edifies itself and moves towards maturity in love (Ephesians 4:16).

Each believer is a gift from God to be used as He chooses (Romans 12:4-8) to enrich the body of Christ, the ekklésia, the church. The ails of the church are numerous; thus, the body is equipped with many gifts, each differing from the next and reflecting God's tailor-made grace to restore, heal, and deliver. The challenge of the gifted is to minister their gifts with the understanding that they are the gifts, anointed to uplift, mend, and restore the body of Christ.

Spiritual gifts empower believers with divinely inspired attributes, and Paul encourages his readers to be prudent in how they administer their gifts. The gifts that God entrusts with us are imparted to demonstrate the favor and love He has towards the body of Christ. His gifts are designed to be complementary, but they can become the source of tension, as with most things entrusted to man.

Gifts can be so polar in purpose that they lie on opposite sides of the spectrum. Some are expressed verbally and others physically. Some are mental and some are spiritual. Some are cerebral and some emotional. God uses both the voice of the prophet and the hands of the minister to express his love. He uses the teacher to increase our understanding, the exhorter to calm our soul, and the giver to reduce our deficits. Leaders govern, and the gift of mercy brings peace and assurance.

Paul did not mention these seven gifts in Romans 12:6-8 to suggest that they are the premiere or the only gifts of the church. These gifts are highlighted to accentuate the main point of the chapter. That is...Be a sacrificial servant of God (v. 1) and overcome evil (the world) with good (v. 21). In the in-between verses, he teaches us that overcoming the world requires a renewed mind, which subsequently transforms our actions (v. 2). We are also cautioned not to think too highly of ourselves because our gifts come from God (vv. 3-5). This is the context in which Paul lists the seven gifts of remediation, gifts provided to remedy our tendency to inflate our self-worth and our inclination towards the temptations of the world.

Figure 8. Gifts of Remediation

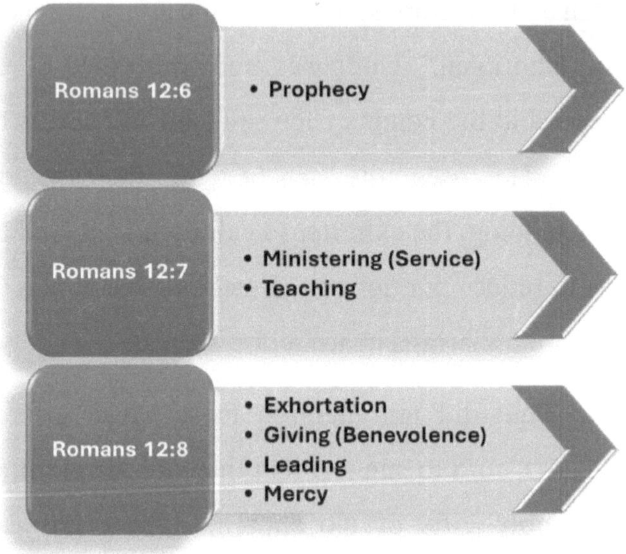

Note: God gifts the body of Christ with the gifts necessary to remedy the issues we face in life.

Unlike official gifts, these gifts are not exclusive. God gifts His servants as necessary to remedy (improve or correct) a situation. Let's take a closer look at Moses for example. Each of the seven gifts of remediation were evident and necessary in his call to lead the children of Israel out of Egypt.

Prophet and Minister

God gifted Moses to be both a prophet and minister. In Deuteronomy 18:15, Moses prophesied the coming of Christ. In Exodus 18:13, he served the people from morning until the evening as judge. As prophet to the people, he brought good tidings. "The LORD shall fight for you, and ye shall hold your peace," he told them in Exodus 14:14 as their faith waivered as certain death collapsed upon them between Pharaoh's approaching army and the Red Sea.

His role as prophet demanded that he disconnect from Israel's situation and look to the future, even though he shared in their current plight. Moses was charged with warning the people that rebellion against God would shorten their stay within the promised land, and they would be scattered abroad (Deuteronomy 4:25-27). Even in their dispersion, God would be working. The purpose of their exile is found in verse 30; they would "return to the Lord." Moses, the disconnected prophet, was commissioned to tell Israel the hard sayings of God, but as a minister, he was approachable even personal.

The gift of ministry or service keenly focuses on finding a remedy for the problems and situations that hinder God's people. This gift was so strong in Moses that he became consumed by it.

It was impractical for Moses to judge the matters of the multitude alone. Moses needed assistance; judging among the people alone was not sustainable, a fact made plain by Jethro, his father-in-law. The gift of ministry drove him to serve others. The people came to him with their issues, and he felt compelled to address them. He saw it as two-fold; he could judge between disputing factions and use the audience to exercise another gift, teaching "the statues of God and His laws." (Exodus 18:16)

Teacher and Exhorter

God gifted Moses to teach Israel His ways and spur them to worship. Moses, the gifted teacher, sought to know, understand, and transfer truth, while the gift of exhortation worked in him to motivate Israel to express their gratitude to God for His mighty acts. Whereas the gift of teaching is cerebral, and the gift of exhortation is emotional, they can work together as a preemptive measure to remedy a predisposition that causes us to drift away from God.

Those with cognitive gifts tend to find less value in emotional impetuses. They generally believe that those who know better will do better. Thus, Moses did not only relay God's message to Israel; he taught them (Deuteronomy 6:1).

After Moses called the Israelites together in Deuteronomy 5:1 to give them the Ten Commandments, he began with the objectives of the lesson, to "learn [the statutes and judgments of God] and be careful to observe them." Then, he gave the motivation of the lesson in verse 2-4, "The LORD our God made a covenant with us... and talked with you face to face." Finally, Moses stated in verse 5 that the children of Israel were afraid of the Lord, so he went up the mountain to talk to God in their stead as his chief qualification to teach the commandments that followed.

Moses stuck to the facts all the way to the conclusion of the lesson in verse 22. His heart towards, relationship with, and deliberate approach to communicating knowledge could also be seen in the way he exercised his gift of exhortation. Both his teaching and exhortation were centered on God and His greatness.

Moses was just as passionate about teaching Israel to worship God as he was about them knowing Him. The gifted exhorter, endowed with a heart of gratitude, is fluent in the art of speaking and singing God's praises. Israel worshiped God for His acts before they knew His commandments.

After seeing God's power against the Egyptians, Israel feared, believed, and sang to Him. Moses led the celebration in Exodus 5:1-2 singing, "I will sing to the Lord, for he is highly exalted. Both horse and driver has hurled into the sea. The LORD is my strength and my defense; he has become my salvation." The song ends in verse 27 with the proclamation, "The Lord reigns for ever and ever."

Moses not only honored the Lord with his words but also with his actions. After telling Israel the words of the Lord in Exodus 24:1-3, he built an altar with twelve pillars, one for each tribe of Israel. The teacher became an exhorter and led the people in making sacrifices in response and obedience to the Word of God.

The cerebral teacher and grateful exhorter can have competing interest in the growth of the body. Whereas it may seem natural for the teacher to maintain that knowing and understanding God should be our chief aspiration, the exhorter can have equal confidence in the importance of joining believers together to worship our great God. However, the gifted teacher and exhorter are well suited to work together to change both heart and mind of those who would otherwise drift away from God and back into the captivities of the world.

Leader and Merciful

People naturally follow those with the gift of leadership, and a merciful leader generally curries favor. The gift of leadership is most apparent in times of uncertainty, and Israel had many. Moses was undaunted by the prospect of facing Pharoah's army who seemingly had them trapped at the Red Sea. He was not dismayed by the lack of food and water within the desert though he knew they were marching through a barren land.

Moses' leadership was unwavering in Exodus 17 where they were overmatched by the army of Amalek. He told Joshua, in verse 9, that he would stand at the top of a nearby hill and raise the rod of God to secure their victory. Moses demonstrated the gift of leadership in helping Israel believe they could defeat Amalek, although the facts as well as the odds were against them.

The gift of leadership tends to be very results oriented. We herald Moses for his wonderful feats of leadership against external threats. However, when Israel murmured, the passions of leadership became misguided. As previously stated, Moses took matters into his own hands and hit the rock when he became distracted by the people's mischief instead of speaking to it as God commanded. This was not the only instance where his displeasure with Israel showed up in his leadership.

In Exodus 32, Moses returned from talking to God and witnessed what God warned. While he was away, Israel built a golden calf and worshiped it. Moses broke the tablets which held the ten commandments, melted the calf, made a stew, and force Israel to drink it (v. 20). It may be difficult to fathom, but this was the gift of leadership exercising mercy.

Moses was not surprised at the sight of the golden calf nor the mischief of the people. We learn in verses 7-14 that God reported the mischief of Israel to Moses and His intent to destroy His people while he spoke with Him on the mountain. The gift of mercy operating within Moses sided with Israel, "And the Lord repented of the evil which He thought to do unto His people." The actions of Moses, forcing the people to drink gold-seasoned water, were influenced by anger but motivated by mercy. His leadership resulted in the people serving an idol, but the influence of his mercy saved them.

Each gift has the power of remediation. Through prophecy, teaching, exhorting, and leading, we combat the anxiety of an uncertain future. Through ministering, giving, and mercy, we bare the infirmities of the weak. One way to discover your gift is to evaluate how God is currently using you.

God has uniquely gifted us for success; we are the remedy for every problem or issue we face. Thus, we don't define success by every micro decision made. Sometimes, the cure can make you feel worse than the sickness. Therefore, we avoid rushing to judgment. Instead, we trust that God is working through us and others by our gifts, and eventually, He will cause us to triumph.

Chapter 6

DEVELOP YOUR TALENTS

Do you see someone skilled in their work?
They will serve before kings; they will not
serve before officials of low rank.
Proverbs 22:29 (NIV)

Talents, the things we learn to do, are gained formally through educational institutions or informally through mentors or self-actualization. Talents are skills acquired over time. Through practice and repetition, we expand our knowledge and improve our understanding. The more knowledge and understanding we obtain and exercise, the more talented we become.

Every believer has skills that make them an asset to the Kingdom of God. God has an inexhaustible demand for readers, writers, speakers, counselors, negotiators, architects, carpenters, landscapers, manufacturers, mechanics, groomers, accountants, bankers, caretakers, scientists, and the list goes on. The beginning of success is realizing we all have skills, and every skill is valued in God's work.

UNFORSAKEN TALENT

When God calls believers out of darkness into His marvelous light, (1 Peter 2:9), He changes our spiritual nature, but essential attributes remain. We become sinners saved by His grace, living life in the newness of life; our lives are changed primarily in the way we live them. Yet, previous history, passions, skills, and aptitudes remain. Paul saw these carryovers from the believer's previous life as beneficial to the Kingdom and encouraged the Corinthians to embrace them.

Paul, in the context of marriage, promoted the idea that those who are called to salvation are not mandated to change their unrelated human conditions (1 Corinthians 7:17). Paul, in 1 Corinthians 7:1-16, provides a lengthy discussion about the relationship between a new believing husband or wife who accepts Christ but now must overcome the challenges of being married to an unbeliever. He admonishes believers that salvation does not justify divorce in such cases. In fact, the potential exists for God to use the new believer to convert the unbelieving spouse.

Salvation, Paul continues, should not be the catalyst for believers to abandon their current state, whether in marriage, circumcision, or servanthood. Believers should abide with God in the same state they were in when He called them (1 Corinthians 7:24). Moreover, spouses were encouraged to remain married, and single people were cautioned against yielding to the pressure of entering a marital relationship. Circumcision was not required for believers, and neither were the circumcised required to reverse their circumcision. Salvation does not free servants from service; the focus of the believer's service graduates from satisfying people to pleasing God. Marriage, circumcision, and service parallel three human relationships; covenant, spiritual, and physical relationships.

Abandoning covenant, spiritual, or physical relationships that preceded our faith in Christ is not a precursor for developing our relationship with Him.

The covenants we've forged with others can become an avenue to share Christ with someone who has not experienced His saving grace. Our covenant, as with marriage, whether it is strong or leaves much to be desired, can bring glory to God if we lead the unbeliever to God or assist in their spiritual development.

Believers need not despise their current relationship with Christ. Jewish disciples wrestled with whether they should force Gentiles to close the cultural gap by adopting Jewish rites. Our relationship with Christ is not founded in rituals of circumcision or the food we consume. Cultural norms, not rooted in sin, can be fundamental to Christian unity and growth.

The spiritual growth spectrum is vast and filled with people with similar challenges. When a believer who understands us accompanies us in our pursuit of Christ, the barriers that work against our spiritual growth become easier to deconstruct. We call this discipleship. A discipling relationship helps expedite spiritual growth by improving our relationship with Christ. In turn, discipleship assists believers in becoming more like Him.

Physical relationships, whether based in Kingdom building or in the world can bring glory to God. For instance, the relationships we foster with the people we work with can benefit God's purpose and plan. Working with talented people will always yield a transfer of skill, and the skills we learn can be used – correction, are best used – in service to God.

A person's talent level is a direct representation of the devotion and commitment to refining the skill. Whether your talent comes from church culture or the absence of it, God wants to use it. He is not simply interested in your gifts but also your talents.

"As for Saul, he made havoc of the church, entering into every house, and haling men and women committed them to prison" (Acts 8:3) under the authority of the chief priests (Acts 26:10-12).

Paul did not hide from who the non-believing Jews trained him to be; he embraced it. He devoted himself to persecuting Christians, "entering every house…committing them [men and women] to prison." (Acts 8:3). He brought the same tenacity to spreading the gospel after he was converted, converting non-believers, and developing Christians.

God does not require believers, with few exceptions, to abandon honorable professions and associations to accomplish His work. He does not despise who we are in the world, He uses who we are to change the world. This does not mean that He is in opposition of servants who desire to rise above their social and economic status, but God abides with believers and uses us in whatever state we are in.

God works within the believer's unique sphere of influence. He uses the people we know and the skills we possess to advance His work and establish His Kingdom. Believers are not of this world; however, those who see their conversion as motivation to prematurely abandon their earthly roles can leave a gap in the world that they were intended to fill.

Paul urged believers to embrace, rather than abandon, their talents. Talents gained before and after Christian conversion can be valuable tools in building God's Kingdom. They should not be despised, rejected, or neglected. When the time we've spent cultivating our talents is called upon, the believer should stand ready and be willing to put their skillful hands to work.

BE FRUITFUL

And let ours also learn to maintain good works
for necessary uses, that they be not unfruitful.
Titus 3:14

It is foolish to hope for accidental success. Success rarely comes to the unprepared and unequipped. Although God is our source and strength, we are more than just inanimate objects manipulated by a master puppeteer. He empowers us to act and perform beyond our natural abilities, but our abilities are what he uses to do so. It is up to us to cultivate the gifts he bestows and the skills we've gained.

David did not wake up one morning to discover he was a mighty warrior. Goliath wasn't defeated by a man untrained in combat. David's fight with Goliath ended in victory because David trained for it. "Bless be the Lord my strength," he sang in Psalms 144:1, "which teacheth my hands to war, and my fingers to fight."

David trained like any other good soldier who prepares for battle. He fought in the same manner he trained. The king at the time, Saul, sought to assist David in preparation for the battle with Goliath by arming him with his armor (1 Samuel 17). David was grateful for the gesture but refused. "I cannot go with these; for I have not proved them," he said. Then, he set out to meet Goliath with a sling in his hand and a few smooth stones in his shepherd bag, which he carefully selected from a brook.

David eventually learned to fight with a sword (2 Samuel 25:13), but he trusted his training more than his weaponry. The fate of Israel and God's reputation rested on the outcome of this battle of uneven foes. David decided to stay within himself and present himself in service to God. He was less concerned about how others thought he should conduct himself in the face of such overwhelming odds. David brought his skills to the battle, and God used his talent with a slingshot to subdue a giant warrior who brandished a sword.

The story of David and Goliath teaches us that God's work requires preparation, and honing our skills is a critical part of the process. God calls on talented believers to do what they are trained to do. Abraham also provides a fitting example of this principle.

Genesis 14:14 says, Abraham "armed his trained servants…and pursued them unto Dan" when Lot, his nephew, was taken captive in Sodom and Gomorrah. Abraham did not give weapons to unschooled men; he enlisted talented fighters for the critical mission of rescuing his nephew. He gave purpose to their natural skill by enlisting them to support a righteous cause.

Without purpose, a talent is nothing more than a hobby. People generally adopt hobbies because hobbies are inherently enjoyable and therapeutic. Hobbies serve as mental, emotional, and even physical escapes from the weighty matters of reality. Because we enjoy our hobbies, we diligently commit time and effort to these leisurely pursuits. Hobbies are not incumbered with the pressure of pursuing perfection but often produce exceptional skills.

With purpose comes accountability and the potential for accountability to counteract the calming effect intended by hobbies. Even so, empowering our hobbies with purpose can bring deeper satisfaction. The demands of purpose can fast-track the arrival of excellence and unlock our talent's capacity to impact the lives of others.

What better way to endow our talents with a higher purpose than to employ them in service to God? Skills gained by earthly means are of immense value in building God's Kingdom. Paul gave an analogy in 1 Corinthians 9:25-27 about athletes and their strict training regiments. Athletes train diligently to win a corruptible crown, but the skills of the believer work toward an incorruptible reward.

If we have purposeful pursuits, our purpose will impassionate our training as we develop and gain new skills. This philosophy fueled Paul's internal drive to avoid wasting his efforts as he trained. He did not "run like someone running aimlessly." He did not "fight like a boxer fighting the air." He trained his body to be disciplined, so his actions could always match his words.

In contrast, the believer who chooses not to use their talents in advancing God's work is like a runner who runs in no particular direction or a boxer who swings at the wind. Skills not surrendered to God can never reach full potential, but those who use their talents (and hobbies) to advance God's work give an eternal value to the time and effort expended in perfecting the capabilities they possess.

Paul understood and appreciated the gifts and talents of his fellow laborers in Christ. This is no more evident than in Titus 3:12-13. Paul resolved to spend the winter in Nicopolis (a city in Cilicia, Thrace, or Epirus) and called on Titus to meet him there with Zenas and Apollos. Paul did not state the reason for his journey to Nicopolis, but we know that Paul's recorded travels served one purpose, to spread the gospel. On this journey, he undoubtedly anticipated the need for a Gentile leader (Titus), a Jewish lawyer (Zenas), and a Jewish scholar (Apollos).

Most scholars suggest that Zenas was either a teacher of the law or a Roman jurist. Beyond this, we are not told much about Zenas. However, his knowledge of the laws of the land, both spiritual and natural, were invaluable to the spreading of the gospel. The constant disputes and tension of the period over the legality of following Christ made Zenas' legal mind a precious commodity.

Understanding the law and how the law related to the gospel was critical in bridging the gap between the saving faith in Christ and the legal mandates of the Mosaic and Roman laws. The book of Acts is characterized by one legal dispute after another. The ministry of Jesus was plagued by the allegations of Pharisees and Sadducees who accused Him of violating the law, both natural and spiritual.

Paul, in the preceding verses (Titus 3:9-11), cautioned Titus to "avoid foolish questions, and genealogies, and contentions, and strivings about the law; for they are unprofitable and vain." Although he advised against entertaining legal questions, he undoubtedly realized that addressing such matters was unescapable and needed Zenas to help in instances where the law was juxtaposed to the grace of God.

Likewise, Apollos was a Jew from Alexandria, a well-spoken scholar of the scriptures (Acts 18:24). Apollos was skilled in synthesizing scriptural texts and presenting them to a captivated audience. We are introduced to him in Acts 18, when he arrived in Ephesus and met Aquila and Priscilla.

Apollos was *instructed* (not gifted) in the ways of the Lord, but his message was founded on a pre-resurrection knowledge and understanding of the gospel. His understanding of the gospel stalled with the baptism of John.

Aquila and Priscilla, who were also laborers with Paul, pulled Apollos aside and *taught* him a "more perfect" way to present the grace of God through Christ Jesus. With Aquila and Priscilla's help, Apollos became a master apologist who publicly refuted his Jewish counterparts, using scripture to prove that Jesus was the Messiah (Acts 18:28).

Paul's final admonishment in his letter to Titus is recorded in verse 14. Here, he promotes the idea that believers must also learn to maintain good works. He undoubtedly included the word "also" to suggest that believers follow the example of Zenas and Apollos who maintained good works. Paul requested the company of Zenas and Apollos because their skills made them useful in gospel ministry. Paul charges us through his letter to Titus to also commit ourselves to developing skills useful in the cause of Christ.

WILLING AND WISE HEARTED

So the number of them, with their brethren that were instructed [or taught] in the songs of the LORD, *even* all that were cunning [or skillful], was two hundred fourscore and eight.

1 Chronicles 25:7

Paul encouraged Timothy to work on the gift of God, which resided in him after Paul ceremoniously placed his hands upon him (2 Timothy 1:6). God gifts believers to fulfill their purpose in the body of Christ, which works to advance God's will and Kingdom in the earth.

Paul's relationship, mentorship, discipleship, and guidance were necessary to cultivate Timothy's skillfulness in using his gifts. For example, Paul instructed Timothy to hold on to the words he spoke and the way he expressed them, in faith and love. This is a great lesson – *How we do* things can be just as important as *what we do*.

Furthermore, the charge to "stir up" the gift cannot go unnoticed. An under-cultivated gift can never reach its potential. Like the talented, the gifted must increase in knowledge and understanding to advance their gift. More importantly, knowledge and understanding are required to teach others. Only God can transfer gifts from one believer to another, but the gifted (and talented) believer can produce talented students.

The construction of the post-Exodus temple holds a remarkable story. Moses, under the commandment of God, asked all the people to bring a free-will offering. With a willing heart, they were asked to bring gold, silver, linen, and skins of assorted colors, oils, spices, and stones (Exodus 35:4-9). The scripture proclaims that "every man and woman, whose heart made them willing," brought an offering to the Lord (v. 29).

It must have been breathtaking to see so many people bringing their resources and skills without regard to who brought more or who brought less. One by one, they answered the call, providing what their neighbor couldn't. Moses gathered the entire congregation of Israel together to request their assistance in constructing and adorning a tabernacle for worship, and they did not disappoint.

With a general call in verse 5, "whosoever is of a willing heart," God gave every person the opportunity to contribute to construction of the tabernacle. The *willing* hearted gifted God with offerings (v. 22), and the *wise* hearted gifted God with offerings and gifts (v. 25). The *willing* hearted brought physical possessions, and the *wise* hearted contributed their possessions as well as their skills.

In verse 30, God singled out two men by name, Bezaleel and Aholiab. These men were unique because they were not limited by a single gift; they had many (v. 33). Perhaps, more importantly, they were not only gifted with wisdom but also with knowledge and understanding. Note that everyone else was simply gifted with wisdom to perform specified tasks. These two men were special because they had wisdom to manage and perform the tasks, knowledge to communicate steps of the tasks, and understanding to eliminate the confusing aspects of the tasks.

Bezaleel and Aholiab were not just gifted, they had knowledge and understanding, which made them qualified to teach others (v. 34). Bezaleel and

Aholiab were skilled at many things, but their ability to teach others multiplied their value in the construction of the tabernacle. They were able to produce talented workers who were also able to devise cunning work. Frustration inevitably finds its way into the efforts of the gifted who attempt to teach others without complimenting their gift with knowledge and understanding.

The gifted tend to underestimate their abilities. They tend to believe anyone can do what they do naturally if they practice "hard" enough. It is common for the gifted to scoff at the idea that they are special in some way. This attitude feeds the notion that everyone has the aptitude to become great or even the greatest at what they do. This simply is not the case.

The gifted, with an aptitude for the arts, can be brilliant in expression but incompetent teachers. Musical savants who can not only play whatever they hear but see what they hear in vivid color can find it difficult to teach others without knowing and understanding music theory. Gifted artists who see every canvas as the perfect surface to weave lines, shapes, and forms together to capture a unique perspective will need to know and understand drawing techniques such as textures, blending, and shadows to set the foundation for aspiring artists. Those with God-given abilities who do not attempt to know and understand how to apply their gifts limit their ability to effectively transfer their skills to others.

Hence, gifts are an aptitude worth cultivating. Like Bezaleel and Aholiab, adding knowledge and understanding to our gifts gives us the ability to teach others. Our aptitude for success is evidenced in the proficiency of our gifts. The believer would do well to refine their God-given skills rather than to rest on them. Success for the gifted believer is to be both gifted *and* talented. Only then can we hope to multiply our hands for the work of the ministry.

Chapter 7

WORK WHILE IT'S DAY

I must work the works of him that sent me, while it is day: the night cometh, when no man can work.

John 9:4

Unfortunately, opportunities can't last forever. Tomorrow will come, and the world will be filled with opportunities seized as well as squandered. For some, today is the last opportunity to make a positive impact whether small or great. The sobering fact is that this could be the last book you'll ever read. Cemeteries are filled with the bodies of people who went to their graves with untold stories, game changing inventions, unrealized potential, and unexploited value. Life should be lived with urgency, as though our tomorrow is not assured but a luxury founded in hope.

Jesus, in Matthew 24 and 25, cautions His disciples not to be deceived at the coming of the end-times. He made four proclamations and used four parables for illustration. He prophesied the destruction of the temple (24:1-4), the rise of a false Christ (24:5-6), the gospel preached to all nations (24:9-14), the great tribulation (24:15-25), and His return to gather the elect (24:26-31).

Next, He illustrated these end-time prophecies with five distinct parables. He explained how the budding leaves of the fig tree served as a sign of summer's approach (24:32-35). He warned His disciples to stay ready for His return because only the Father knows the day and time; His return will be as the era of Noah when the flood came unannounced (24:36-51). The kingdom of heaven was compared to ten virgins, five wise and five foolish – the foolish did not bring enough oil to sustain their fire until the bridegroom arrived (25:1-13). Then, He explained the kingdom of heaven in relation to a wicked and slothful servant (25:14-30). Finally, He described His return using the symbolism of a shepherd who separates the sheep from goats to illustrate His intent as King to separate the righteous from the unrighteous (25:31-46).

Each parable has the same theme or moral of the story; we should not be complacent in our preparation for Jesus' return. The opportunities we have today may not be accessible tomorrow, or we may not be available to take advantage of them. This sense of urgency guided Jesus in His earthly ministry.

> I must work the works of him that sent me, while it is day: the night cometh, when no man can work. As long as I am in the world, I am the light of the world.
>
> John 9:4-5

In John 9:4-5, Jesus seized the opportunity to manifest the power of God by healing a man who was blind from birth. Healing the man on the sabbath day gave the Pharisees justification to scrutinize the event, but the urgency of the moment outweighed the pressures of Jewish politics and religious constraints (John 9:13-34). Jesus did not act because His power was infinite; He healed the blind man because His time on earth was limited.

WELL DONE

Success is the fruit of those who live with urgency, using their gifts and talents rather than burying them.   In the fourth end-time parable mentioned above, the Lord in the story gave talents to three men (Matthew 25:15).   The servant who received five and the servant who received two talents doubled their talents by investing with exchangers. These, the Lord called good and faithful servants.   The servant that received one talent, the wicked and slothful servant, buried it.

These talents were literally a weight of a substance used as currency; however, the parable affords us the occasion to think of the talents given to the servants symbolically in terms of a skill. Matthew 25:15 states, "The Lord gave talents "to every man according to his several ability."   The number or measure of talent given to each servant depended on their aptitude for managing resources. The Lord knew his servants well and distributed more talents to those who would make the best of the time allotted.

The wicked and slothful servant could not appreciate the urgency nor expectations of his Lord's return. The fear of failure paralyzed him to the point where he wasted the opportunity to invest his talent in something or someone that could produce a return.

Instead, he determined to "play it safe," leaving his talent idle, buried in a hole until his Lord returned.

This parable highlights two types of servants. Although one servant received five talents and another received two, they were both considered the same. The amount of talents given nor the increase delivered distinguished them in the eyes of the Lord. They both were told "Well done, good and faithful servant" (v. 22). They proved themselves to be faithful, reliable, and trustworthy over what they were given. In contrast, the wicked and slothful servant was an unprofitable servant (v. 29). The talent given to him was wasted. Time passed while the Lord was on his journey; however, neither the talent nor the servant grew because they were both idle.

CURRENCY OF LIFE

Consider currency for a moment. Every nation operates on a currency. America has its dollar, Mexico has its peso, Europe has its Euro, and Djibouti has its franks. One's financial worth is measured by how much money (liquid or assets) they have. Their financial security, however, is defined by how they manage and/or spend their money; do they waste it, invest it, reallocate it, or save it. Time has similar properties to money; it is the currency of life.

The value of one's life is measured in years, months, days, and hours. How we spend our time is a key factor in measuring the significance of our life. Do we waste it, invest it, or reallocate it?

Everyone wastes money and time. Money and the time we spend to get it gives us power to purchase the wisdom, creativity, labor, skills, and resources of others. The extent to which we define these purchases as necessary is highly subjective and situational. Is gambling a waste of money and time? Some people see gambling as an exhilarating pastime while others find themselves trapped by its addictive nature and decline to poverty. Is sleeping a waste of time? How much sleep does the body need? Solomon said, "wake up though sleepy head lest though come to poverty" (Proverbs 20:13). Even oversleeping is a waste of time.

Like money, time cannot only be spent but invested. One of the best ways to grow financial resources is through investments. Investing money takes it out of your hands and connects it with someone or something that has the potential to produce future gains.

> Therefore, my beloved brethren, be steadfast, unmovable, always abounding in the work of the Lord, knowing that your labor is not in vain in the Lord.
> 1 Corinthians 15:58

Time is not tangible; thus, we cannot expect to add a single sunrise to our lifespan by investing it. Although bodily exercise and a proper diet are investments that have the potential to extend our days, the best investments will produce gains long after we are gone. Therefore, invest time in activities, people, and causes that will outlive you.

When we invest in ourselves, we gain the knowledge, understanding, and skills necessary to increase our effectiveness. Time invested in sermon preparation improves how the preacher communicates the gospel of Jesus Christ. Time invested in prayer and Bible study prepares believers to perform the ministries of edification and reconciliation.

Have you ever experienced a life-changing speech, talk, or conversation? Did you walk away thinking, "that was time well spent?" The person allotted a few minutes of their life to invest in you by unpacking the experiences they gained over time. The event or conversation only lasted a moment, but the time they sacrificed remains alive in you.

I am extremely grateful for the time my grandparents invested in me, frequently pausing to impart the wisdom of their years. Their colloquialisms and sage advice continue to echo in my ear. Sadly, I cannot seek their counsel today, but my actions are often influenced by the fruitful words they planted during my youth. Is there a greater return on investment than knowing our impact on others will outlive us?

The modest lives of my maternal grandparents were not enviable compared to the financially affluent of their time. They raised ten children on a fixed income and many of them struggled and in some cases yielded to the temptations made strong through poverty. Some of their children sought success through ill-gotten gains and others worked hard to forge a *better* life.

Regardless of the path taken, my uncles and aunts always looked out for my best interest. Even those who made questionable decisions refused to allow me passage on the road they traveled. My formative years were largely shaped by the way they shielded me from the corrupt lures of life.

Therefore, the value of their lives is not simply an accumulation of their personal successes and failures. By encouraging me to follow them in righteousness or pushing me in the opposite direction of their regrets, they taught me that our true worth is not found in our temporal actions but in how we shape the next generation in the time we are allotted.

Life Is But A Vapor

The currency of life is a gift given to every person in equal measure on a minute-by-minute basis. The number of minutes lived on earth differs from person to person. Additional time cannot be earned, unused time cannot be traded, and excess time cannot be saved. Therefore, we must remain cognizant of how we manage the few moments we are granted to live in this world.

Every life is a gift from God. By "life," we mean "zōē," the Greek word used in John 1:4 indicating both physical and spiritual life (Strong's 2222). John, in the preceding verses, establishes that Jesus (the Word) existed with God in the beginning as the content of creation and source of life. Within Him was the power to create physical life and grant humanity the gift of eternal life.

Life, both physical and spiritual, is a gift from God, and how we live it is our gift to Him. This is especially true for those who confess and profess Jesus as savior and live by faith. All who live (in Him) no longer live unto themselves; instead, they live unto Him who died for them and rose again (2 Corinthians 5:15). Our level of gratitude for the purchase of our freedom from death (Romans 8:2) is demonstrated in how we spend the currency of life.

"Life is but a vapor," James 4:14 says, "that appeareth for a little time, and then vanisheth away." The uncertainty of our days and the limited time we have on earth pressures us to sure-up our journey and avoid dead-end paths. Each person maximizes their time on earth by being in the right place, doing the right thing, for the right reason. The right place is where we are until God moves us. The right thing is what we are gifted and called to do in the season God chooses to use us. The right reason is because God has placed each of us in a designated place for a given purpose to glorify Him and edify His people. No one knows what tomorrow holds, so we must do whatever we can while we can.

Life on earth is short when compared to eternity. This fact makes time our most precious commodity. Therefore, we should make the best use of it. Why waste time focusing on petty differences, arguing about issues that will not matter in five years? It is more beneficial to invest our time in things that have a generational impact so your contributions and work can outlive you.

Time continuously progresses forward. Even though we are constantly looking for ways to save time, it marches on with or without us. Time cannot be saved; it can only be reallocated. We can be more efficient or waste less of our time, but even that does not truly save time. A more efficient and judicious use of time affords us the opportunity to allocate more time to things we would otherwise not have time to accomplish. The wise use of time is an investment in things that bring a return. This is the principle advocated by Paul to the church of Ephesus.

> See then that you walk circumspectly, not as fools but as wise, redeeming the time, because the days are evil. Therefore, do not be unwise, but understand what the will of the Lord is.
>
> Ephesians 5:15-17

Paul encouraged the early church to walk as wise disciples of Christ to "redeem the time," or be more efficient and judicious with their time because evil was pervasive. The key admonition for the Ephesians not to be unwise with their time is to "understand what the will of the Lord is." When believers focus on understanding and performing the will of God, they will redeem their time by investing in things that have eternal implications.

Paul understood that he was called to minister Jesus Christ to the Gentiles, so he journeyed through Philippi, Ephesus, Thessalonica, Antioch, Corinth, Rome, and others, investing his time in spreading the Gospel message. When he was immobilized by his various imprisonments, he did not wait until he was released to continue his ministry. He redeemed time by writing letters.

Paul's example teaches us that redeeming the time means making the best use of the time God grants independent of your present condition. He didn't attempt to live the life he desired. He lived within his reality, investing his gifts and talents in a manner best suited for the moment. His ministry was defined by the will of God. He was not called to travel the world but to spread the Gospel to the Gentiles (non-Jews); his travels were a means to fulfill his calling. Paul invested his time in something (the Gospel) and someone (Timothy and Titus) that would outlive him so the power of God that worked in him could bring glory to God in the church by Jesus Christ throughout every age (Ephesians 3:20-21).

Gratitude for the gift of life is best demonstrated in how our time is spent. The value of our lives will be measured by how they impact current and future generations within our sphere of influence. A life worth living demands that we limit wasteful moments, invest in those who will finish what we began, and allocate time for things with the greatest potential to have a positive impact on our relationship with Christ and His people. Just as Jesus invested in His disciples so that their lives would have greater meaning, we should express a similar love towards those we have the privilege to disciple.

BIBLIOGRAPHY

Britannica, The Information Architects of Encyclopedia. "ontology". *Encyclopedia Britannica*, 28 Dec. 2024, https://www.britannica.com/facts/ontology-metaphysics. Accessed 15 June 2024.

Easton, M. G. (1897). *Illustrated Bible Dictionary (also known as Easton's Bible Dictionary)*. 3rd. London: T. Nelson & Sons.

OpenAI. (2024). Copilot [Microsoft Edge] https://www.microsoft.com/en-us/edge/copilot.

Lang, C. (2003). *The Time is Now: Doing the Best with What You Have.* Washington: Pleasant Wood.

Santayana, G. (1905). *The Life of Reason: The Phases of Human Progress.* https://www.gutenberg.org/cache/epub/15000/pg15000-images.html.

Strong, J. (1800). *The Exhaustive Concordance of the Bible.* Cincinnati: Jennings & Graham.

UNESCO. The World Atlas of Languages. UNESCO, https://en.wal.unesco.org/world-atlas-languages. Accessed 8 January 2024